The **PocketScroll**® Series

SHAAR PRESS

A
SHAAR
PRESS
PUBLICATION

In
loving memory
of
our mothers

חנה בת בהיה ע״ה
Ann Haber ע״ה

and

שמחה בת ג׳מילה ע״ה
Sylvia Serouya ע״ה

who taught us
to
never look down

Rabbi CHAIM P. SCHEINBERG
Rosh Hayeshiva "TORAH ORE"
and Morah Hora'ah of Kiryat Mattersdorf

הרב חיים פינחס שיינברג
ראש ישיבת "תורה אור"
ומורה הוראה דקרית מטרסדורף

I have personally known Rabbi Michael Haber, of Congregation Ohel Yaacob of Deal, New Jersey, for a number of years. I am very pleased that he has written the book, *Don't Look Down,* and that it will be published by Artscroll/Mesorah Publications.

I urge all to read the book, and feel that it will be quite beneficial. I am certain that it will be well accepted, and will motivate and inspire all who read it to enhance their observance of Torah and *mitzvot.*

To Rabbi Haber, I give my blessing, that he continue to inspire our people through the written and the spoken word. May he continue to publish works which educate and elevate Jewish people throughout the world. And, may he and his wife see much Torah *nahat* from their children and grandchildren.

רחוב פנים מאירות 2, ירושלים, ת.ד. 6979, טל. 537-1513 (02), ישראל
2 Panim Meirot St., Jerusalem, P.O.B. 6979, Tel. (02) 537-1513, Israel

Table of Contents

Acknowledgments

Many of the essays in this book have followed a similar path: from *speech* to *article* to *book*.

The *speech*, typically, would be a Shabbat speech in our beloved congregation, Ohel Yaacob, in Deal, New Jersey, where I am privileged to serve. The *article*, based on the speech, would be in "Image" magazine, in which I am privileged to write. The *book*, of course, is the volume which is before you.

Much credit for this publication must go to my good friend, Jack A. Kassin. As Jack and I discussed the concept of a book, he expressed the hope that it would inspire personal growth and character improvement. He sought a book which could be discussed at the Shabbat table by parents and children and which would be fuel for personal growth based upon our holy Torah. It is my hope and prayer that this volume meets those expectations.

I would like to thank Rabbis Scherman and Zlotowitz for their confidence; Rabbi Avrohom Biderman for his belief in this book and for his constant words of encouragement and support; and Yossi Haddad for his selfles help with this project.

Additionally, I would like to thank Mrs. Nina Indig for her incredible editing. Much of the crispness of the writing and the consistency of its logic are due to her efforts.

Much credit must be given to Ben and Rochelle Matsas of "Image" magazine for printing my articles in their publication and for their sincere desire to spread Torah knowledge to the Jewish world.

As always, I would like to thank my wife, Molly, for her support and encouragement. She shares in any success which my published works have had.

Sincerely,
Menahem Haber
4 Rachamim Ellul 5761

Don't Look Down

STRIVING FOR EXCELLENCE

In a familiar scene in the world of cartoons, a character is being chased. He runs and runs, with the chaser in close pursuit. Suddenly, the character reaches a cliff. Unaware, he continues to run – first on the cliff, then past it.

As could only happen in a cartoon, the character is able to keep running, with only the air beneath him.

After a while, he looks down. He sees that there is nothing under him. He realizes that, according to the laws of gravity, he should not be where he is – that he does not belong there. At that moment, he falls to the ground.

∞ ∞

Sometimes, in life, the greatest obstacle to success is *not* the individual's limitations. Rather, it is the feeling that he or she "should not" succeed. As long as the individual *believes* that success is attainable, he or she could aspire to great heights. If, however, that same individual believes that he or she "should not" succeed – if the person "looks down" – failure is practically assured.

Recently, a friend told me about a colleague of his. The man, a newcomer to their industry, was having great success in his sales during the summer – even though summer is the slowest season. The man "did not know any better." Since nobody told him that he should fail, he succeeded.

In 1953, Roger Bannister ran a mile in less than four minutes (3 minutes, 59.4 seconds). In the forty-seven years since then, the record has only dropped by about fifteen seconds. One has to wonder: Are there, perhaps, people out there who, physically, could run a *three-minute* mile? Are they limited only by their belief that such a thing is not possible?

Indeed, to a great extent, our success is limited by our own expectations. This applies to almost any avenue of life – sports, medicine, finance, and (this is our subject) the spiritual dimension of our lives as well.

∞∞

When Moses sent spies (*meraglim*) into Canaan, they returned, stating (*Bamidbar* 13:33):

And there we saw the nephilim, the children of giants …
And we were, in our eyes, like grasshoppers.

It is no surprise that their conclusion was (*Bamidbar* 13:31):

We cannot conquer that nation, for they [its people]
are stronger than we are.

When one is, in his or her own eyes, as small as a grasshopper, it is likely that he or she, like the spies, will use the word "cannot." If you believe that you are limited – *you will be.* If, however, you ignore the naysayers (whether they are external or simply the voices within you); if you do not "look down"; if, rather, you place your faith in G-d and make the proper effort – you can exceed all expectations.

Though humility is one of the hallmarks of our people, pessimism is not. There is nothing Jewish about feeling that you must fail, or even that you must be average. We must strive for spiritual excellence. We must strive to inject as much holiness into our lives as we possibly can.

Alei Shur, the contemporary *mussar* classic, states (I:168):

Every person must know that he or she has importance.

There, *Tanna D'Vei Eliyahu* (Ch. 25) is quoted:

A person must ask, "When will my deeds reach the
level of the deeds of Abraham, Isaac, and Jacob?"

Abraham, Isaac, and Jacob? My deeds? Should we set our sights that high?

Alei Shur continues:

> *Whenever one does not set his sights upon perfection,
> it is very difficult for him to attain it. When one does
> set his sights upon it, however, it is easily attainable.*

To underline this concept, we need only to consider some of the luminaries of our past and the obstacles they overcame: Joseph (sibling rivalry; alien environment); Moses (speech impediment); Rabbi Akiva (began Torah study at an advanced age); Onkelos, author of the *Targum* of the Torah (a convert); and more.

If any of them would have thought that he could not possibly excel, he would have assured his own failure. Instead, each set his sights upon perfection – and attained it.

Do *you* strive for spiritual excellence? Do you set your sights as high as they could be set? Do you ask yourself: *When will my deeds reach the level of the deeds of Abraham, Isaac, and Jacob?* Do you seek to achieve as much as you possibly can, in the performance of all *mitzvot?* Do you set high goals for yourself in both the commandments between man and G-d (such as *Shabbat,* family purity, prayer, *kashrut,* and Torah study) and the commandments between man and man (such as charity, helping others, and playing a leadership role in *chesed* projects)?

Remember: If you believe that you will fail, you probably will. If, however, you believe that, with G-d's help, you can succeed and even excel, you are on your way. Set your sights high — and *don't look down*.

Our Violin

LOVING TORAH AND *MITZVOT*

The small town was surrounded by desert. To reach the town, a traveler had to withstand intense desert heat. Most travelers, consequently, dressed in light clothing and carried little with them. Still, by the time they arrived, they were visibly exhausted and thoroughly drained of strength.

One day, an unknown traveler came to town. On his back, incredibly, was a violin housed in a heavy hardwood case. Yet, despite his load, the traveler arrived fully refreshed, invigorated, and full of life.

The people were puzzled. They asked, "Other people carry as little as possible, yet arrive here totally exhausted. You carry a heavy load upon your back. Despite this, you are refreshed and full of life. How could this be?"

The traveler responded, "Traveling is lonely. On my journeys, I often find myself to be down in spirit. So I stop, remove the violin from its case, and play. And I feel better. The music sustains me. The violin is the source of my strength."

He continued, "I must, therefore, correct your statement. It is not that I am refreshed *despite* the violin on my back. Rather, I am refreshed *because* of it."

∞∞

Observant Jews accept the Torah, and the *mitzvot* which accompany it, as basic components of their lives.

Yet some view their observance as follows: *Life is a struggle. Add to this the requirements of Torah and mitzvot, with their countless commandments and restrictions, and the struggle becomes more intense. However, I am willing to sacrifice. This is what the Creator requires of me. So I will bear the burden. And I will make it through life despite it.*

This attitude is missing something.

It is admirable to accept obligations. It is admirable to be willing to sacrifice. And it is admirable to stand ready to carry out the Will of the Creator.

However, Torah – its *mitzvot*, its faith – must be viewed in a different light. The *mitzvot* sanctify us, refine our character, make us into better parents, better husbands, better wives, better children. Our faith sustains us, providing us with the strength we require to withstand times of trouble.

∞∞

Let us draw an insight from the life of one of our forefathers. Jacob made an agreement with Lavan, his future father-in-law. Jacob would work for seven years, and Lavan would give him Rachel as a wife.

The Torah states (*Bereishit* 29:20):

> *And they [the seven years] were in his [Jacob's] eyes as a few days, because of his love for her.*

There is a question here: Shouldn't it be the opposite? Because of Jacob's love for Rachel, the time should have seemed endless. How do we explain that it was "as a few days"?

The commentary *Bechor Shor* explains: Jacob knew what Rachel was, and he felt that seven years was a small price to pay. He felt that he was receiving something of great value in return for very little effort — that he was getting the better part of the arrangement — so he fulfilled his obligation with enthusiasm.

In doing *mitzvot,* we must feel much the same as Jacob felt in working to marry Rachel. We have a contract with the Creator. We must view our role as a privilege, not an obligation. We are getting "the better part of the arrangement." The work we do is little in comparison to the returns we receive from it.

Let us not simply feel this way ourselves; let us convey this attitude to others. As we carry out the *mitzvot,* let us do so with the animated enthusiasm of a person who feels blessed to have them. Even when things in life appear to be difficult, let us make it known that this is our joy, this is our privilege.

Torah is not a burden. *It is our violin*.

Windows

TAKING ADVANTAGE OF OPPORTUNITY

Windows open and windows close.

At Cape Canaveral they speak of a "launch window." This is the limited segment of time during which a spacecraft can begin its journey. Within this period, conditions are favorable – the "window" is open. Once this time has passed, however, conditions are not as favorable. The "window" has closed.

A while ago, I entered a convenience store to make a purchase. Usually, customers expect to spend only a few minutes in such stores. They enter, pick up a few items, pay for them quickly, and leave. On this day, however, it was different. At the checkout counter, there was a line of people – approximately twenty of them – standing single file. *A line of people*. What was going on?

The answer came soon. The cashier announced, "Whoever is *not* waiting to purchase a lottery ticket, please come to the front." Only a few people came forward. They were *not* waiting to purchase lottery tickets. Apparently, everybody else was. The prize that week had risen to thirty-five million dollars.

To the people on line, the wait was worthwhile. This was, in their minds, an opportunity. It would not always be there.

The window would soon close.

Think of your life as a window. While it is "open," you have the opportunity to do *mitzvot*. Once it "closes," that opportunity is gone.

The following classic parable of the sainted *Chafetz Chaim*, of blessed memory, vividly makes the point:

A man, struggling to earn a living, heard of a distant island where the streets were filled with diamonds. He sailed there to find that the valuable gems were indeed everywhere. He collected some.

After some time, he learned that the island people valued something else: fats. He began to collect them, eventually stockpiling fats in great measure.

Proud of himself, he sailed home, bringing along the fats he had collected, and the few gems he had amassed.

Only later did he realize what he had done. He had squandered an opportunity. His chance had gone. Now it was too late.

That island is this lifetime. And the diamonds are *mitzvot*. Once we return "home," our chance to collect them is gone. The window of life will, by then, have closed.

Now, break that larger window of life down into many smaller windows. Every individual window – every small segment of time – affords us a unique opportunity. We can do the right thing – or we can do the opposite. We can choose what is spiritual and permanent – or we can choose what gives us momentary pleasure or immediate satisfaction, as per this incident (*Bereishit* 25:29-32) in the lives of two famous brothers:

> *Jacob prepared a meal. Esau came back from the field. He was tired. Esau said to Jacob, "Pour me, please, from this red substance, for I am tired ..." Jacob said, "Sell me, today, your birthright."*

Now, we must point out that the birthright brought with it something quite important: the mantle of spiritual leadership.

And so, Esau was presented with a window. He could elevate himself. He could choose the spiritual (the birthright) over the physical (the food) – or he could not.

The Torah reveals his thought process:

> *"Behold, I am about to die. Why do I need a birthright?"*

Esau was *not* about to die. However, his immediate physical desire – his hunger – had overcome any thoughts of spiritual elevation. To Esau, the food was far more important than the birthright.

The window had opened and the window had closed. And the opportunity to do something that was spiritually elevating had disappeared.

∞∞

As I recall, the following was told of the Steipler Rav, *zt"l*:

One day, this great sage was seen walking to the synagogue. Once he arrived at the building, he paused, and waited outside for a brief time. Then he entered.

He was asked why he had stopped. He answered that it was his practice to review a full tractate of Talmud each time he walked to the synagogue. This time, he did not complete it by the time he reached his destination. So he waited outside until his review was done.

Which tractate do *you* review on your way to the synagogue?

Every hour, every minute, every second of every life is an opportunity. Are we using our time to elevate ourselves, to inject a healthy measure of *kedushah* (holiness) into our lives and the lives of the members of our families? Or are we letting opportunities pass – and letting windows close?

∞∞

We can take an important cue from an incident in *Megillat Esther*.

After the decree against the Jews was announced, Mordechai, through a messenger, asked Esther to approach the king to plead for the lives of the Jewish people. At first she hesitated. Mordechai then sent another message to her. His words (according to the translation of *Ibn Ezra*) were (*Esther* 4:14):

> *"Who knows, perhaps for this very moment, you became queen."*

In other words, she was placed in a certain spot, at a certain moment, to fill a role. She had a mission to fulfill. She could do so, or not.

Of course, she did – and the rest is history.

Though usually not as dramatic, missions exist for us as well. Each of us has not one, but many missions to fulfill. Each encounter, each conversation, each meeting is not just something trivial – it is an opportunity. However, it may be an opportunity that will not return. Here, now, take advantage of it. Ask yourself, "Why am I here, in this spot, at this moment, with these people?" Then act accordingly, while it is still possible.

Our message, therefore, is this: Life is a window, and encounters are windows as well. Like the folks waiting in line for the lottery tickets, we have an opportunity that we must take advantage of. Let us act while the opportunity is there.

Because windows open. And windows close.

The Attic of Your Mind

TAKING ACTION

There is an attic in your mind.

L ike all attics, it is out of view. Items are placed there, then ignored. Things come in, but never go out. There is dust. There are cobwebs.

In your mind's attic, there are many things:

- suggestions (never made);
- words (never spoken);
- ideas (never brought to fruition);
- advice (never imparted to others).

Why?

Because you had second thoughts:

- that the suggestions would not be warmly received;
- that the words would not be accepted;
- that the advice would go unheeded.

So you kept them to yourself "until further notice," as you told yourself. Now they gather dust – *in the attic of your mind.*

༜

Let us go to the Torah (*Bereishit* Ch. 37) for guidance. The brothers of Joseph plotted to take his life:

> *"Let us kill him ... and we will see what will be of his dreams."*

But Judah stepped forward, saying:

> *"What will we gain by taking the life of our brother, and concealing the act? Let us, rather, sell him [as a slave] for he is our brother, our flesh."*

Judah's brothers heeded his advice, and sold Joseph into slavery. Following this event, the Torah states:

> *And Judah descended from among his brothers.*

At first glance, this appears to be a simple, physical description: he went from a place of high altitude to a place of low altitude.

Rashi, however, based on a *Midrash*, views this differently: The brothers of Judah demoted him. The descent of Judah was a descent in stature. They said to him:

"You said, 'Let us sell him' – and we listened to you. Had you said [instead], 'Let us return him to his father,' we would have listened to you."

"We would have listened to you!"

One wonders: Did Judah indeed consider advising, "Let us return him to his father"? Might he have entertained the thought, only to later smother it because, he reasoned, *they would never accept it?*

∽⊱

Return, now, to the present, and shine the light of this insight upon your own attitudes, relationships, and encounters. Recall the suggestions and the advice which you considered giving, but did not. Perhaps one or all of the following rings true:

Spiritually: A friend or relative has distanced himself from Torah. There are few *mitzvot,* there is no study, there is no *kedushah* (holiness). His life has become one without meaning. You know that a healthy measure of Judaism would turn his life around. You consider stepping forward, but then you have second thoughts. *He'll never listen,* you assume. So you keep your ideas to yourself.

Socially: She's "seeing" somebody, seriously. However, she's been serious before, but was unable to

— 27 —

make a commitment. You feel strongly that this match is a good one, and you're concerned that she might once again let it pass. You consider expressing your opinion, but you decide not to.

Financially: He's about to enter into yet another business venture that is, in his mind, certain to succeed – and in your mind, certain to fail. You would like to raise objections, but on second thought, you decide not to intervene.

Parentally: You watch closely as she raises her daughter, and you do not like what you see. *But*, you say, *I'm not perfect either*. So you disqualify yourself from speaking out.

In all these instances, and in similar ones, it is time to rethink your decision to do nothing. Are you certain that "they'll never listen"? Is it possible that you are indeed in a position to have an influence? Is it possible that your advice would be heeded, and that you could very well turn a person's life around?

Is intervening constructively not better than encountering the chilling words, expressed after it is too late: *"I would have listened to you!"*

Consider, then, expressing the words you have smothered. Use them to improve others. Do not let them gather dust – *in the attic of your mind.*

One Hundred and Twenty

MAKING THE MOST OF LIFE

In *Parashat Vayeilech* (*Devarim* 31:2), Moses addresses the Jewish people prior to his death:

"I am 120 years old today."

Each of us should wonder, "How will I view my own life as I look back at it in my old age?" With this in mind, we present:

One Hundred and Twenty

I am 120 years old. My life has been long and interesting. I have seen much, done much, met many people, and traveled far and wide. My experiences have taught me a great deal.

Through the years, I've changed. The outlook of this old person is worlds apart from the outlook of the same person when young. If only I could relive my life! Knowing what I know now, I would do things quite differently …

• *I would revisit every Shabbat of my adult life.*

Oh, I observed *Shabbat* – no question about it. I did not work, nor drive, nor open lights. So much, however, was missing! My observance was mechanical and dry. There was no feeling, no joy. There was no holiness. The opportunity to grow as a family was ignored. The chance to enhance the spiritual component of our lives was squandered. The day that could have elevated us was allowed to pass, practically unnoticed.

■ *I would take back my prayers and recite them over.*

How powerful our prayers are:
- The *Amidah (Shemoneh Esrei)!* With three steps forward, you stand before your Creator. You expose the inner stirrings – *hegyon libi* – of your heart. It's you and your Creator, and nobody else.
- The *Shema!* Its six-word first sentence, *"Shema Yisrael Hashem Elokeinu Hashem Echad (Listen, Israel, Hashem is our G–d, Hashem is One),"* represents more than a statement of faith. It is the classic declaration of courage uttered by the lips of our martyred ancestors.

My own prayers? I did recite them. In fact, I hardly ever missed. But there was no feeling, no emotion, and no holiness. My heart and my lips were miles apart.

■ *I would relearn all of my Jewish studies.*

Talmud Torah keneged kullam – the value of Torah study is immeasurable. I would go back to every class. I would reread every page. I would cherish every letter.

■ *I would take back some of my spoken words.*

I would take back *many* of my spoken words. Why did I say those things about people? What did I gain? Why did I disparage others? Why did I hurt them? Was it to make me feel better about myself? Was it to feed my own insecurities? I've done great damage. My pain is too great to bear.

■ *I would bring my parents back.*

This time, I would give them the respect they deserve. This time, I would give them the love they deserve. This time, I would let no day go by without expressing my feelings toward them. Have *you* hugged your parents today?

■ *I would make my children young again.*

I would set a better example. I would never forget that they learn as much from what I do as they learn from what I say. I would find the time to at least ask, "How was your day?" I would even listen to the answer. I would encourage them – this time – to study Torah even beyond their school years. I would make certain they are close to a rabbi.

■ *I would revisit every encounter with a friend.*

My main focus would be different. It would not be, as it always was, "What can I gain?" Rather, it would be, "What could I do for you?" I would ask, "How are you?" – and mean it. I would learn to listen. I would learn to hear cries for help – even if the words are not spoken. I would be truly happy when my friends succeed. I would go out of my way to speak to the person who is neither powerful nor popular. I would think about doing *chesed* (kindness) wherever I went.

■ *I would express my admiration to life's hidden heroes:*

- to the middle-income Jewish father, who would not compromise his honesty — despite the pressure of earning a living;
- to his wife, who teaches her children what many people say but few really believe – that your value in life is not measured by financial success;
- to people who work hard at being good husbands, good wives, good parents, or good children;
- to good friends.

At age 120, most of my life has passed. I cannot revisit the years gone by. If you are younger than I, however, your life is before you. You can direct it upon any course you choose. Regarding every action, ask yourself :

- Will I someday regret this?
- Will I someday wish I had done something else?
- Will I someday say, *"I would ..."?*

A Bag of Cookies

GIVING IS RECEIVING

The young man waited in the airport lounge for his plane to depart. He found a seat and reached for the bag of cookies that he had purchased a few moments before. He removed a cookie, and placed it into his mouth.

Just then, something astonishing took place. The elderly man seated next to him placed *his* hand into the bag, removed a cookie, and placed it into *his* mouth. The nerve! There was no "please," no "thank you." The man just helped himself.

Then it happened again. The young man took a cookie, and the old man took one, too. Again, no "please." Again, no "thank you." The gall!

This sequence continued until only one cookie remained. Then the old man, incredibly, picked up the cookie, split it in two, gave one portion to the young man, and took the other for himself.

The young man was appalled. However, his flight was being called, so he stood up and reached for his valise. As he did so, something fell to the floor. It was a bag of cookies — unopened.

Now he realized what had taken place. This bag was the one that he had purchased. The one that he had eaten from was the property of the old man.

☙❧

The young man is us.

As we do *mitzvot*, as we conduct ourselves in the manner that the Creator has set forth for us, we often feel as if we are the givers. We sacrifice, we strive, we summon all the dedication we can muster in order to do what is right. *Oh*, we think, *how we sacrifice! Oh*, we think, *how we give!*

But, like the young man, we are mistaken. For when we conduct a life filled with *mitzvot*, we benefit. Like the young man, we have not given. *We have received*.

The Torah states (*Bereishit* 1:26 and 2:7):

> *And G-d said, "Let us make a man – in our form, our image" ... And He blew into his nostrils a living soul.*

The body requires nourishment, and the soul does as well. It craves spiritual sustenance. It longs for holiness. It thirsts for purity.

The Torah states (*Devarim* 32:46-47):

> *And he [Moses] said to them [the people of Israel], "Put your hearts into all the words I have commanded you [to follow]… for this is not something empty for you. Rather, it is your life."*

When an individual lives a life devoid of a spiritual dimension – when the only commitment is to physical and material pleasure – the soul starves, and an enormous vacuum exists. There is a palpable sense that something is missing. This is life without meaning.

When you do mitzvot – do you give, or do you receive?
Note this statement (*Ruth Rabbah* 5:9):

> *More than [the giver] does for the needy person, the needy person does for the giver.*

When you carry out acts of kindness, acts of *chesed*, pause for a moment to consider the individual whom you have helped:

- When you help the poor, picture the person you have helped now having a real dinner.
- When you visit the sick, look into the eyes of the person whose spirits you have lifted.
- When you help a family, consider what you have done for its children.

The sense of fulfillment is immeasurable.

When you do mitzvot – do you give, or do you receive?

Glance at a newspaper. Consider the status of the world around you. Think about its values – or lack of same. Think about indecency, dishonesty, and the acceptance of depraved behavior. Think about the erosion of family.

We believe (*Tehillim* 144:15):

> *Fortunate is the nation of which it is so; fortunate is the nation whose G-d is Hashem.*

Now, think about *mitzvot*. Think about *Shabbat*, about holidays. Think about prayer. Think about the study of Torah. Take measure of what they have done for you. Take measure of what they have done for your family.

As the Torah states (*Devarim* 5:26):

> *If only their hearts would be so – to fear Me and observe all of My mitzvot – always. This will be good for them and for their children – forever.*

When you do mitzvot – do you give, or do you receive?

Think about your life. Think about its spiritual components. Think about Torah, about *mitzvot*. And, as you do the *mitzvot*, ask yourself: *Have I given, or have I received?*

The answer is quite clear. The cookies you ate were not yours. You have given nothing. *You have only received.*

"*Seder*" of the Mind

LIFE LESSONS FROM THE PASSOVER SEDER

*K*adesh *Urchatz* is the beloved mnemonic chant which helps us to remember the sequence of activities of the Passover *Seder*. Each word, or set of words, represents one of the sixteen procedures which comprise this special evening.

In our lives as Jews, there are concepts, principles, and ideas which we must draw upon constantly, and never forget. They make us better. They inspire. They motivate us to grow.

We present here a number of such ideas – in *Kadesh Urchatz* order. This is, in effect, a *"Seder* of the mind."

KADESH. *Sanctify*. Understand that even the most ordinary activities can be made holy. When one eats or sleeps with proper intent, he or she is serving the Creator. And, of course, even a simple encounter between people is a challenge and an opportunity to do good. *"Kedoshim tihyu* – be holy" (*Vayikra* 19:2). Sanctify each moment.

URCHATZ. *Wash*. Wash away self-doubt. Eliminate any thoughts, any inner voices, which tell you that you cannot grow, you cannot do more, and you cannot elevate yourself to a higher level of observance. Recognize that your potential is unlimited. Drive yourself by asking, as our Sages (*Tanna D'Vei Eliyahu*, Ch. 25) implore us to, "When will my deeds reach the level of the deeds of my forefathers, Abraham, Isaac, and Jacob?"

KARPAS. *Dip the celery, or whatever vegetable you use, into salt water or vinegar.* Feel the pain of the many individuals who need your help. Mentally, "dip" into their difficulty. "Experience" their hunger, illness, loneliness, poverty, and lack of self-esteem. Avoid the temptation to blame them for their problems. Just understand.

YACHATZ. *Break the middle matzah, and put aside one piece until later.* There is much that we would like to accomplish in life. The committed Jew is constantly driven. There is improvement necessary within, and there is much to do for others. We become discouraged: "I will never finish. Should I just give up?"

In answer, we quote Rabbi Tarphon (*Avot* 2:16): *"The work is not your responsibility to complete; you are not, however, permitted to avoid it."* Like the middle matzah, "break" your goals into components. Do what you can at once. Then, do what you can later. You may never fulfill all of your goals, you may not do all that you would like to do – but you *can* make a substantial difference.

MAGGID. *Speak*. Talk to others. Take advice from them. Speak to sages, parents, and friends. Learn to listen. *"The ways of a fool are proper in his [own] eyes, but the one who heeds advice is wise" (Mishlei* 12:15).

RACHTZAH. *Wash*. Wash away imaginary obstacles. There is no shortage of reasons for doing nothing. Obstacles can be overcome. It is a matter of attitude. *"The path of the lazy [appears to him as] a fence with thorns, while the path of the righteous [appears to him to be] clear" (Mishlei* 15:19).

MOTZI, MATZAH. *Recite the blessings, eat the matzah*. Recognize what the matzah represents – instant change. First our ancestors were slaves. Then, suddenly, they were free. There was no time for the dough to rise.

Discouraged about life? Afraid that things will never change? Fear not. Look at the matzah, and understand what it represents.

MAROR. *Bitter herbs*. Life is not all sweet. It has its difficulties. It has its tensions. At times, the pressure is quite intense.

Let us understand that we do not see the entire picture. Let us recognize that the Divine Plan is beyond our understanding. And let us keep in mind the classic statement of the sage, Ben Hei Hei, *"According to the difficulty, so is the reward"* (*Avot* 5:22). This applies to the *actual* reward, and it applies to personal growth. We are tested by adversity, and we grow from it. Let us rise to every challenge.

KORECH. *Eat the matzah and maror together.* "Sandwich" yourself among good people. A good friend — or, rather, a friend who is good – motivates and inspires by example. You are challenged, constantly, to advance, to progress, to elevate yourself.

"What is the best path a person should take?" Rabbi Yochanan ben Zakkai asked. Rabbi Yehoshua answered (*Avot* 2:9), *"A good friend."*

SHULCHAN ORECH. *Set the table.* The Jewish code of law is the *Shulchan Aruch – The Set Table*. Whatever you do, let it be within the framework of our laws and traditions. We, ourselves, cannot know what is best. We must let our laws and our traditions be our guide.

TZAFOON. *Find what is hidden.* Do not give up on people – look for their *hidden* strengths. Help them reach their potential.

BARECH. *Bless*. Bless the Creator for giving you the strength, resources, and ability to do *mitzvot*.

HALLEL. *Praise*. Praise the Creator for enriching your life with the beloved laws of our Torah.

NIRTZAH. *It has been accepted*. May our prayers be fully accepted. Remember to pray, always. Pray on behalf of your children, pray on behalf of your parents and friends.

May the stirring of our souls penetrate the heavens. And may we constantly pray to grow as Jews, as we daily motivate ourselves ... with this *"Seder* of the mind."

The Whiskers of a Mountain Lion

COMMITMENT

The woman went to the wise man. She was concerned about her marriage.

The wise man said, "If you want to have a better marriage, bring me the whiskers of a mountain lion."

The woman had confidence in the wise man, and dutifully resolved to carry out his request. In fact, she knew of a mountain that was inhabited by a lion. However, the creature was quite ferocious. She therefore laid out a careful plan to fulfill her mission.

She climbed the mountain, bringing with her a bowl of food. Carefully, she placed the bowl down, and ran. She was not seen by the lion.

She did this for three days. Each time she returned, the food was gone. The lion had eaten it.

A few days later, she took the next step. She again brought a bowl of food. This time, however, she let herself be seen by the lion as she was leaving. This procedure, too, she followed for three days. Again, each time she came, the food from the day before was gone.

Then she went further. She carried the bowl in her hands to the lion. She placed it down before him. Now trusting her, the lion ate. This, too, she did for three days.

On the third day, while the lion was eating, she took a pair of scissors, cut a few of the lion's whiskers, and brought them to the wise man.

He said to her, "These whiskers are the key to a good marriage. If you would just invest the same effort into your marriage as you did into acquiring these whiskers, your relationship with your husband would flourish."

∽∾

Most of us care a great deal about Judaism. We care a great deal about our observance of *mitzvot*. And most of us fully intend to grow, advance, and improve.

Incredibly, though, we are very much like the woman in the above story and her attitude toward marriage. We want results, but we do not make the effort. We are unwilling to sacrifice. We lack true commitment.

Yet, in other areas of our lives, we have plenty of commitment. We *are* willing to sacrifice. After all, we "remove whiskers from mountain lions" all day long. We do so in business and in our professions. We set goals. We have meetings. We evaluate performance. We work hard to succeed. We are committed.

Now, compare this to our religious commitment. Do we set religious goals for our families and ourselves? Do we ever have meetings to discuss them? Do we ever sit down with rabbis to evaluate our progress?

The fact is, most people – even those who fully appreciate Judaism and are otherwise quite committed to it – do not put into it the same planning and effort they put into their businesses. The spiritual progress of most people is practically left to chance, with no goals, no planning, no evaluation, no order.

Now, let us make another comparison – not to business, but to leisure pursuits. How seriously people take their hobbies! They purchase the best equipment. They take lessons. They practice. They rise early in the morning to get an early start.

How many people can say the same about their pursuit of Judaism?

When the Torah instructs us regarding animal sacrifices, it states (*Vayikra* 1:2):

If a man from you brings a sacrifice.

Regarding this, the *Midrash* (*Hachefetz*) states:

[The Creator states,] "When people bring a sacrifice and it is slaughtered – and its blood is sprinkled upon the altar – I view it as if [it is 'from you,' as if you have given of yourself, as if] you have sacrificed your own soul."

This is what we must be ready to do.

When an individual brought a sacrifice he was, in spirit, connecting to his forefather, Abraham, and to Abraham's supreme act of devotion: his willingness to sacrifice his son.

Now, let us note the comments of the *Gemara* (*Berachot* 20a) on the subject of sacrifice and commitment.

Rabbi Pappa said to Abaye, "Why were miracles done for earlier generations – yet miracles are not done for us?" He [Abaye] answered, "The early generations gave their souls to sanctify the Name of G-d. <u>We</u> do not give our souls to sanctify the Name of G-d."

If, on some level that is beyond our understanding, the generation of Rabbi Pappa was lacking in its dedication – what can we say about ourselves?

Yet we do know how to sacrifice. We do know what commitment is. It is very much present in other dimensions of our lives.

Let us put in the effort — as we do in other dimensions of our lives – constantly, successfully, *"removing whiskers from mountain lions."*

Face the Music

ACCEPTING RESPONSIBILITY

The military is known for its strict rules of conduct. In days of old, military men who broke the rules braced themselves to hear their sentences. As their fates were being announced, instruments were played. A soldier who misbehaved would do well to prepare himself to *face the music.*

In our spiritual lives, many of us find ourselves doing anything but facing the music. Deep down inside, we are often unwilling to sincerely evaluate ourselves, afraid to confront the conclusions we may reach (especially if those conclusions involve admitting wrong). We therefore make mistakes and compound them, unwilling to make the changes which a sincere look at ourselves would bring.

∽∽

The brothers of Joseph are prototypes of this concept. To them, Joseph was a dreamer. His "delusions of grandeur" (as they viewed his dreams) would never materialize. They sold him into slavery.

Over two decades later, the brothers and Joseph crossed paths again. By then, Joseph had indeed risen to a position of prominence. At first, the brothers did not recognize Joseph, and he did not reveal his identity to them. Eventually, Joseph did reveal his identity to his brothers. The Torah states (*Bereishit* 45:3):

> *And his brothers could not answer him, because they were astounded.*

In an instant, the brothers realized that they had erred. Their thoughts about Joseph were mistaken. *He was right – and they were wrong.*

It's a frightening thought: You can convince yourself of something, and maintain that conviction for many years. Yet, had you been honest with yourself, you could easily have seen that you were mistaken.

The *Midrash* (*Bereishit Rabbah* 93) compares Joseph's encounter with his brothers to an encounter which each of us will have after "one hundred and twenty":

> *Rabbi Shimon ben Elazar, in the name of Rabbi Elazar ben Azaryah, said that Abba Kohen ben Delayah was accustomed to saying: "Woe unto us on the day of judgment ... Joseph was the youngest of the brethren, yet his brothers could not withstand his reproach. As it says, 'And his brothers could not*

answer him.' When the Holy One, Blessed Is He, will
reproach each of us ... how much more so ..."

"When the Holy One, Blessed Is He, will reproach each of us!" When we will have no choice but to face the music, will the mental structures we have built to justify our actions come tumbling down?

☜☞

Is there something we can do about those mental structures now? Yes, if we have the courage to face the music.

There are two obstacles to doing so.

(1) *Lack of desire:* How much does an individual really desire to uncover his or her faults?

The *Siftei Chaim* writes:

> *Since an individual does not desire to see his faults and what is lacking, he actually does not look for them, nor recognize them, so how could he turn away from them?*

People are not honestly searching for their faults (as opposed to the faults of others. We'll search for *them*, anytime!).

(2) At times *it is genuinely difficult to know oneself.*

A number of years ago, a study was done. Groups of six people were asked to spend time together, completing a variety of tasks.   At several intervals, the people were asked, "In your opinion, what do the others in the group think of you?"

Needless to say, many of the responses were inaccurate. A person is often unaware of the impression which he or she is making upon others. We've lived with ourselves for years. But often, others know us better than we know ourselves.

How, then, can we discover what we are lacking?

First, much of it is obvious. Most of us have glaring faults that we know full well could and should be improved. If we have the desire to find them, we will.

Second, we can speak to others. How many people have ever sat down with their rabbi to evaluate their progress? To identify areas which need improvement? To discuss *mitzvot* which are being overlooked?   What about discussing things with family members?   Your husband or your wife, your father, your mother – probably all have something to say about you. Yes, it could be unpleasant. But we're here to grow, to advance, to elevate our levels of holiness – not to stand still.

The *Siftei Chaim*, quoting Rabbi Yerucham of Mir, writes:

> *When a person has a decision to make, if he has no wise man to consult with, he should discuss it with anybody, even a layman. Of course, he need not follow the advice of the other person. But he should at least hear an opinion.*

Let us each, therefore, ask ourselves these questions:

- Am I ready to sincerely search for my faults, and to proceed to correct them?
- Am I ready to acknowledge the mistakes which I have made for years?
- Am I really satisfied with my level of observance?
- Do I perform the *mitzvot* with the same energy that I do other things?
- Have I brought sufficient Jewish spirit into my home?
- Am I doing all that I can as a parent?
- Am I doing all that I can as a husband, as a wife?
- Does the study of Torah play a prominent role in my life?
- Does my *Shabbat* table feel like one?
- Have I allowed bad habits to control my life?
- Have I spent enough time with my parents?
- Are my prayers what they should be?
- Do I sincerely care about others?

Let us not hesitate. Let us uncover our faults, lay them out, and conquer them.

Let us *face the music.*

Little Did They Know

THE MAGNITUDE OF SMALL DEEDS

On an ordinary day in the 18th century, a culinary tradition was born. As legend has it, an English nobleman found himself with a bit of an appetite. To satisfy it, he requested something new: a helping of meat between two slices of bread. To this day, the delicacy bears the name of this nobleman. He was the Earl of … Sandwich.

In the Civil War, the two competing armies were led by a number of well-known military men. Among them was General Ambrose Everett Burnside. The general was a bit different in his grooming preference – he allowed whiskers to grow on the side of his face. This style was named after him. First, the whiskers were called *burnsides*. Later, they came to be known as *sideburns*.

Each of the two men was doing something in innocence. Their thoughts were only for then, not for the future. They had no idea that their deeds would live on. *Little did they know.*

What holds true for the trivial, in this case, is doubly true for the sacred. Let us turn to the holy thoughts of our Sages for insight.

In the *Midrash*, the Sages muse about three personages of the Jewish past: Reuven, the son of Jacob, our forefather; Aaron, the brother of Moses; and Boaz, a leader in Israel during the era of the *Shoftim* (Judges).

First is Reuven. His brothers intended to take the life of Joseph, their brother (*Bereishit* 37:20):

> *"Let us kill him."*

Reuven, without revealing his true motive, dissuaded them (*Bereishit* 37:22):

> *"Do not spill blood. Throw him into the pit."*

His covert intention was to save Joseph, to return him safely to his father.

Commenting on this, our Sages (*Vayikra Rabbah* 34) state:

> *If Reuven had known that [the Torah would record his actions], he would have carried him [Joseph] on his shoulders and brought him [safely] to his father.*

Second is Aaron, older brother of Moses. Aaron is told by G–d (*Shemot* 4:27):

> *"Go to meet Moses in the desert."*

He does.

> *And he went, and he met him ... and he [Aaron] kissed him [Moses].*

This was a genuine, noble act from one whose younger brother will overshadow him. Commenting on this, the *Midrash* states:

> *If Aaron had known that [the Torah would record his actions], he would have come out to meet him [Moses] with cymbals and dance.*

Third is Boaz: revered, respected, a leader. Noticing the plight of Ruth – a convert, a stranger in need – he provided her with food. Commenting on this, the *Midrash* states:

> *If Boaz had known that [his actions would be recorded in the Book of Ruth], he would have brought her fatted calves and fed them to her.*

> *Little did they know.*

Step back for a moment and take in the full picture. All of the actions captured by the *Midrash* are admirable. Reuven, Aaron, and Boaz all displayed enormous strength of character. They were equal to the tests which they encountered. Yet, our Sages insist, *they might have done more if they knew they would be in the book.*

Let us return to the *Midrash* for its remarkable conclusion. The Sages ask:

> *Now that there are no prophets, who writes about our actions?*

The answer:

Eliyahu HaNavi [Elijah the Prophet] records them all.

There's a message here: When you expect a deed to be forgotten, when you feel that its effects will pass, you invest little effort in it. However, when you know that the deed is being recorded, when you are conscious that it is being frozen and preserved, you are infinitely more careful.

Let us delve a bit further into the nature of this "book."

In his prayer on behalf of the Children of Israel following the worship of the Golden Calf, Moses stated to G-d (*Shemot* 32:32):

> *"If You forgive them [You forgive them], and if not, erase me, please, from Your book that You have written."*

Commenting on this, the *Sefer Meyuchas* states:

> *"From Your book" [means] from the Book of Life, which You have written.*

The *Midrash HaGadol* explains it more figuratively:

> *Does He have a book? Does He write in a book? Rather, this is to tell you that everything is exposed and known to Him.*

The Rambam (Maimonides), in his commentary on *Avot* 2:1, has a similar explanation:

This [the idea of a book] is the language of the Torah,
to teach us that all needs are known before G-d.

Whether the book is literal or figurative, the message is the same: Everything is recorded. Everything is important. Nothing is trivial.

Before we act, before we brush off a deed because we view it as being of no consequence, we must ask ourselves: How will it appear in the book? A conversation, a comment, an expression, a smile, a frown, a grimace, a stare, a glance, a motion, a gesture – *they all have meaning*. And they have permanent impact.

Consider all of this before you act. Be aware of the significance of every deed. Let it never be said about your actions that ... *little did you know.*

I Remember

THANKING THOSE WHO
HAVE HELPED US

A recent headline, on one of the inner pages of my local newspaper, caught my attention:

Woman Interned in W.W. II Finds, Thanks, Rescuers

According to the article, 1400 Americans and other foreigners were held prisoner by the Japanese during the war. On August 7, 1945, U.S. paratroopers, in a daring rescue, came in and liberated them.

In 1985, forty years later, one of the former captives – a woman who was 12 years old at the time of the rescue – took action. She obtained a U.S. Government document that had been, by then, declassified. It listed the names of the seven men who took part in the mission.

With years of effort, she located all of the men (by then in their 70's) who were still alive, and the widows of the men who had passed away. Her purpose? To express her gratitude. "It's never too late to say thank you," she said.

ᴄᴏᴏᴄᴏ

Here's a question, possibly a painful one: How much effort do *you* make to thank the people who have helped you? How hard do *you* try to say, "I remember!"

After all, our holy writings make quite a case for doing so.

When Jacob, our forefather, had his fourth son, the child's mother, Leah, declared (*Bereishit* 29:35):

"This time, I thank God."

Consequently, she called him *Yehudah* (Judah), from the Hebrew root which means *to thank*.

The *Midrash* (*Bereishit Rabbah*, 98) states:

Rabbi Shimon bar Yochai said: "Nobody says, 'I am a Reuveni'[from the tribe of Reuven], 'I am a Shimoni' [from the tribe of Shimon]. Rather, people say, 'I am a Yehudi' [from the tribe of Judah]."

A Jew is a Yehudi. We are the "People of the Thank You." *We remember.*

Let's examine how far our tradition carries this concept.

The first three of the ten plagues inflicted upon the Egyptians were the following:

- *The water turned into blood.*
- *The ground brought forth frogs.*
- *The ground brought forth lice.*

Regarding these plagues, we have a question: Why was Aaron, rather than Moses, commanded to bring these plagues? Why was it he who waved his staff over the water (for the first plague) and the earth (for the second and third)?

The *Midrash* (*Midrash Rabbi Eliezer,* 19) answers:

> G-d said to Moses, "The water, which guarded you when you were placed in the river [as an infant], and the earth, which protected you when you slew the Egyptian [and buried him in the ground because he was beating a Jew] – I will not allow to be smitten by you."

The lesson: We owe something to those who have been good to us. *We must remember.*

Our Sages call this *hakarat hatov*, acknowledging the good. But why do they only speak about *acknowledging* the good? Why not carry it a step further, and discuss *repaying the good?*

A possible answer: Repaying the good (even if done with words only) is indeed our ultimate aim. A primary obstacle in doing so, however, is the failure to recognize that good was done to us in the first place.

Perhaps many of us are in denial:

- *Did that person really help me?*
- *Would not things have worked out anyway?*
- *Somehow, wouldn't I have been fine?*

Call it pride. Call it ego. Call it self-esteem. Something inside convinces us that we've done it alone. So there is no acknowledgment of the good. No "Thank You." No *"I remember."*

But we are the "People of the Thank You"! And *hakarat hatov*, acknowledging the good, is too rooted in our tradition, too important, to allow our egos to smother it. If it takes an internal struggle, so be it. We're ready.

In the life of King David, there is a simple incident (*Shmuel Bet*, Ch. 19) that underlines this concept.

During difficult times, Barzilai the Giladi, a man of considerable wealth, sustained the king and his men. Once the king was in a better position, he was determined to acknowledge and repay the favor. So he offered to sustain Barzilai.

A person of lesser commitment than King David would not have bothered. A king has a great deal to do. Could he be expected to remember everything?

It's a simple slice of Jewish history. But it's a lesson for every Jew.

∽∾

A friend of mine, then a young man, had a close relationship with a rabbi. The older man had done much to help and influence the younger one – as he had done with other young people. My friend felt that he owed much to the rabbi. So he bought him a simple present, accompanied by a "thank you."

The rabbi cried! He said, "In all these years, you are the first person who thanked me."

Take five minutes. List the people who have played major roles in your life. Your parents, of course. Perhaps a teacher of an early grade who had great influence. A friend who was there for you during times of distress. A rabbi; a business mentor whose advice put you over the top; a doctor who helped you get better. Your husband or wife, of course.

If finding some of these people takes a search (which would probably be no more than two or three phone calls), it is well worth the effort. They extended themselves for you. You, therefore, could extend yourself for them.

How should you thank them? With a gift, with a card, with words. Anything is enough, as long as you show that you did not forget.

Remember: We are the "People of the Thank You." Part and parcel of our holy tradition is acknowledging the good, *hakarat hatov.*

"It is never too late to say thank you."

It is never too late to say, *"I remember."*

Left Field

COPING WITH FRUSTRATION

Professional sports have done considerably more for us than simply providing excitement and entertainment. They have added to the vocabulary of the English language. After all:

- When an opponent is close to defeat, he is considered to be *on the ropes* (boxing).
- When somebody expresses criticism after the fact, he is a *Monday morning quarterback* (football).
- And, if an individual truly desires to be thorough, he had better *touch all the bases* (baseball).

Then there is the sports metaphor used to describe the unexpected, the surprising, those events which occur without warning. Our sports-inspired description of them is that they've come *out of left field*.

We often make great effort to do good, to help others. Perhaps we try to "match" a young man and young woman together; to find employment for an individual who needs it; to "make peace" between two people in conflict.

We make the effort. But despite feverishly intense work on our part, success is beyond our grasp. Our efforts end in failure.

So the "match" you put together went nowhere fast. The position you recommended to that out-of-work individual was not for him. And your efforts at peacemaking were not embraced by either of the feuding parties.

You tried. But you failed.

Hold on! There's another piece to the puzzle. Very often, once you are out of the picture, positive results take place. Something happens. Surprisingly – *out of left field.*

- The young man and woman, who were not " right" for each other, each meet and marry somebody else.
- The person seeking employment somehow receives a lucrative offer which he accepts instantly.
- And the feuding individuals – uncharacteristically – decide to bury the hatchet, and are now the best of friends.

You're happy, but you're sad. You're happy that all ended well, but sad that your efforts played no role.

Let's turn to the Torah for guidance.

Among the holy objects of the *Mishkan* – the traveling

Temple which our people constructed in the desert – was the *Menorah* of gold. Although Moses was given specific instructions for the construction of the *Menorah*, he was unable to carry them out.

Rashi (on *Shemot* 25:31) informs us what transpired:

> *Since Moses had difficulty with it, G-d told him, "Throw the talent [of gold] into the fire, and it will be formed of itself."*

Moses did so, and the *Menorah* was indeed formed … *of itself*.

This explains why the Torah does not state, "And you [Moses] shall construct the *Menorah*," since it was not to be crafted by Moses, or by other human hands.

Fine. This, however, raises a question: If G-d's intent was, from the outset, to construct the *Menorah* through a miracle, why did he allow Moses to struggle with it first? Why let him try – only to fail?

The Maharal of Prague, in his commentary *Gur Aryeh*, provides the answer:

> *All actions which come from Above require effort from man below.*

In other words, the effort of Moses was not unrelated to the final success of the project. In fact, Moses' seemingly abortive actions were a prerequisite to the completion of the Menorah.

Effort by man below is necessary before the blessing of success is bestowed from Above, even if that success appears unrelated to the effort – coming *out of left field.*

In a similar vein is a comment by Rabbi Chaim of Volozhin on a well-known statement of the *Gemara.*

In the *Gemara* (*Megillah* 6b) it is stated:

> *Rabbi Yitzchak said: "If a man tells you, 'I made the effort but did not find,' do not believe him. 'I did not make the effort, and I did find,' do not believe him. 'I made the effort and I found,' believe him."*

Rabbi Chaim notes: When somebody makes an effort, he does not describe the results of his actions as a "find." He considers the results to be an achievement. The choice of words of the *Gemara*, however, is intentional. Even when a person makes the effort to study, the moment of insight is a gift from the Creator. It is a "find."

The same is true in other dimensions of our lives: that "match" which did not work, the job connection which did not bear fruit, your efforts at peace which seemingly went nowhere were all first steps toward success. We may not have been able to connect the action to its result, but the connection may very well be there.

Therefore: If your effort to do good appears to be *on the ropes*, don't be too harsh on yourself. Don't be a *Monday morning quarterback*. Just be certain that you've *touched all the bases*. Then say a prayer, and look for success – *out of left field.*

Lame Ducks

TAKING INITIATIVE

He is a lame duck.

The connotation is quite harsh. But the phrase speaks volumes.

The term refers to a political figure whose term is approaching its end. Perhaps he or she was voted out of office. Or, perhaps, he or she was ineligible to run again. Or, maybe, a retirement was announced.

Though officially this person is still in power, he or she is severely limited. After all, everybody knows that somebody else will hold the position in the near future.

Lame ducks are not limited to the political arena: There are, for example, *lame-duck parents*. There are *lame-duck children*. And there are *lame-duck friends*.

How did these individuals lose their power? Through a lack of initiative, and the inability to take action.

We turn to the Torah (*Bereishit* 11:31-12:1) for guidance:

> *And Terach took Abram, his son, Lot the son of Haran, his grandson, and Sarai, his daughter-in-law, the wife of Abram, his son, and they went with them from Ur Kasdim to go to the land of Canaan. They went to Charan and stayed there. And the years of Terach [when he died] were two hundred and five. And Terach died in Charan. And G-d said to Abram, "Go forth from your land and from your birthplace and from your father's home to the land which I will show you."*

Abraham, our forefather, left his birthplace, together with his father, Terach. They stopped in the city of Charan, where Terach died. Abraham continued on to Canaan, the future land of Israel. Apparently, Abraham left Charan to go to Canaan *after* his father died. So it seems from a casual reading of the text – which is never enough.

Let's take a second look:

When Abraham was born, his father was 70 years old. Seventy-five years later, Abraham left the city of Charan, to go to Canaan. According to these figures, Terach was 145 years old at the time (70+75=145). Yes, he was old. *But he was not dead*. In fact, Terach lived for another sixty years, leaving the earth at the ripe old age of 205. So, for a full sixty years of Abraham's sojourn in Canaan, *his father was still alive*.

Yet there is no mention of interaction between the two men. While Abraham (then called Abram) was developing into a spiritual giant, Terach was out of the loop, stepping away from his responsibilities. In effect, *Terach was a lame duck* — as are others, who step away from the responsibilities of their position. They are what they are *in name only*.

There are lame-duck parents —

- who make no effort to arm their children with Torah and *mitzvot*;
- who allow their children to slide down the academic ladder, without taking action to reverse the decline;
- who know their offspring are with the "wrong" group, yet look away as if unaware;
- who allow their teenager to purchase a car – before he or she is mature enough to use it;
- who permit their child to host a party, with alcohol for all, until late at night;
- who never praise, only blame.

There are lame-duck children – older children, married, with families of their own —

- whose elderly parents need their help, but never receive it;
- who always *intend* to visit, but never get around to it;

- who do have feelings of love, but never express them.

There are lame-duck friends —

- who ask, "How are you?" but would rather not know;
- who can never listen, because they're always speaking;
- who see a friend in need, and expect *others* to help;
- who never correct a friend, because it may be unpleasant;
- who detect a mistake about to happen to a friend – in marriage, in business, in *anything* – yet remain silent.

Are you a *lame duck* in any of your life's roles? Or do you step forward, take initiative, and get things done?

Whatever the position in question – president, mother, father, son, daughter, or friend – there are some who take action, who exercise initiative, while others step back passively.

Which are you?

Take action. Seize the moment. Don't be inactive. Don't be *a lame duck.*

Notches

MEASURING SUCCESS

It did not take very long for the visitor to notice that every man in the village wore a thick black belt. Observing more closely, he became aware of an additional detail: the belts had notches scratched into them. Some belts had many notches; others had only one or two. What did it all mean?

He posed the question to a native of the village, who explained, "The more notches a person has earned, the more respect he deserves."

"Very interesting," replied the visitor. "And how, may I ask, does one earn his notches?"

"Well," he was told, "we villagers place great value upon skill in trapping. Before us, our fathers were trappers, as well. Our tradition is very strong. For each creature that a person traps, he is permitted to give himself a notch. So when you see somebody whose belt is filled with notches, you are seeing somebody of great worth. He has earned the respect of others."

Just then, a native of the village strode by. His belt was filled with notches. The visitor followed him, anxious to observe a skilled trapper in action. What he saw, however, was not quite what he expected.

The villager approached a struggling dove. Its wing was broken, and it was unable to fly. The villager set its wing, nursed the dove back to health, and released it to fly away. Then the villager took a knife, and scratched a notch into his belt. The visitor was puzzled. This was not trapping. Why the notch?

The villager now approached a rabbit. It had entangled itself in a dense rosebush, and could not get free. The man spread the branches apart, gently removed the rabbit, and sent it on its way. Again he took a knife, and scratched a notch into his belt.

The confused visitor could not contain himself any longer. He approached the villager and requested an explanation. These are the words he heard: "As you may know, this village reveres skill in trapping. The notches in a trapper's belt bring him great honor. But I am not in agreement with this. After all, trapping is, essentially, a selfish act. The person is doing something only for himself. He deserves no special respect.

"Setting a creature free, on the other hand, is something else. It is an act of giving. When I do this, I feel good, because I have done something unselfish. So I reward myself with a notch."

෴

Too often, in the "village" that is this world, honor is accorded to people who do not deserve it, and withheld from people who do.

Just pause, for a moment, and ponder the public perception of success. When you hear the words "He is very successful," what do you think? That he has completed many acts of kindness? Of course not. This accolade is understood to mean that he is financially secure.

As Jews, however, we view life and success quite differently. We judge ourselves, not by how much we have acquired, but by how much we have imparted to others. You've helped somebody? You've done an act of kindness? You've given? You're successful! *Scratch a notch into your belt.*

The critical role that giving plays in the life of a Jew can be learned from *Devarim* 23:4:

> *Neither an Ammonite, nor a Moabite, may "come into" the congregation of G-d.*

This means that males from the nations of Ammon and Moab, even if converted to Judaism, may not marry Jewish women. Why not?

The Torah continues (*Devarim* 23:5):

> *... because they did not provide you with bread and water when you left Egypt.*

Though we've had more bitter enemies, Ammon and Moab are singled out because of their miserly nature. This is not what we, as Jews, are about. It is the antithesis of Judaism. It is the opposite of giving.

After all, what did Abraham's servant seek, when searching

for a wife for his master's son, Isaac? He looked for a woman who would say, "Drink, and I will give your camels to drink, as well." *He sought a person with the desire to give*.

This, then, should be our outlook. Giving is the name of the game. This should govern our deeds – but it is easier said than done. In fact, it's difficult.

Here are two reasons why:

(1) *Our environment*. Society places many pressures upon us. There is pressure to be attractive (from peers, from parents, from husband or wife). There is pressure to earn a living. But there is little pressure to do good. One who leads a self-centered life will feel little pressure to do otherwise.

(2) *The nature of the mitzvot of giving*. Many *mitzvot* are not governed by time. There are no deadlines. One could easily let a week pass without visiting anybody who is ill. One could miss opportunities to help a friend, advise a relative, or give encouragement to a peer. Since there are no deadlines, we might easily think that we will do it tomorrow. So we let the opportunity pass. It is, therefore, all the more critical that we develop self-discipline. It is imperative, once we understand the importance of giving, that we take practical steps to fit it into our life-style. We must do this. It is too easy to overlook.

Remember. In the village that is this world, respect is often misdirected. Respect the givers. Become one of them. *And place a notch in your belt.*

"I Didn't Know You Would Catch Me"

INTEGRITY

All was not well in the forest.

Winter was approaching, and the creatures which dwelled outdoors had thought they were well prepared. At the advice of Wise Owl they had planned ahead, scurrying to and fro as they gathered food for the upcoming freeze.

But now the food was not there. It had been stolen! And Wise Owl knew exactly who the culprits were: Sly Fox, Cunning Snake, and Cuddly Puppy.

Wise Owl summoned the suspects to his tree. He sternly peered at the alleged perpetrators as he began his interrogation.

"Why did you take the food?" he asked Sly Fox.

"I didn't know that it belonged to anybody," was the reply.

"Why did *you* take the food?" he asked Cunning Snake.

"I didn't know that stealing is prohibited," came the reply.

The owl turned to Cuddly Puppy. "And why did *you* take the food?"

"I didn't know —," began Cuddly Puppy.

"Continue," said Wise Owl.

"I didn't know — that you would catch me."

As is the case with the creatures of the forest, so is often the case with their human counterparts.

Many people are exceedingly concerned about their public image. People in positions of prestige, especially, painstakingly cultivate their public persona, seeking to project a detached aura of dignity. But when nobody is looking – when negative activities will either be overlooked or tolerated – the person is often very different. If there is no pressure – from those in positions of authority, or from peers – there is no self-discipline.

"I didn't know that you would catch me."

This brings to mind "The Great Snowball Incident of 1995." On December 23 of that year, the New York Giants faced the San Diego Chargers in a football game. The contest was apparently not entertaining enough for some of the fans who were present in the stadium that day. So they conveyed their displeasure by throwing snowballs at people on the field. By the tens they hurled them. An equipment man was struck by a snowball and knocked unconscious.

Who were those snowball throwers? Were they prisoners on furlough from a local jail? Were they federal parolees? Not quite. Among those involved were doctors, lawyers, and a chief of police.

What happened? What of the dignity with which these people normally conduct themselves? Whither their sterling character and impeccable conduct?

I didn't know you would catch me.

We turn to the Torah for guidance (*Devarim* 27:15-26):
The Levites cried out:

"*Cursed is the man who ...*"

Eleven transgressions are listed, including these:

- "*Cursed is a man who makes a graven image ... and places it in secret.*"
- "*Cursed is the person who makes light of his father and mother.*"
- "*Cursed is the person who moves the property line of his friend.*"
- "*Cursed is the person who smites his friend in secret.*"

Question: What do the above transgressions have in common?

Answer: *They are all done in private.*

The Torah recognizes the ways of man. Not uncommon is the individual who projects a refined image in public, yet exhibits depraved behavior in private. Moreover, what we refer to as "private" is not limited to actions that are literally not seen by others. It includes deeds that are indeed seen, but not frowned upon. When certain misdeeds are widely practiced, they become accepted. There is no public displeasure with the person who performs these actions. It is as if nobody saw.

The Torah states its displeasure with the private sinner in no uncertain terms. Even if nobody saw, or nobody cared, know that your Creator sees — and cares.

Each of us must ask: *How much internal strength do I have? If nobody will ever know, would I do it? If nobody cares – if everybody does it – would I participate? Or do I have the character to do the right thing – to fulfill the Will of the Creator – even if nobody cares?*

Think about life. And think about what takes place after it. Those who motivate themselves, who aspire to elevate themselves level after level, will be proud that they stood strong. Others, having passively gone along with the tide, having "thrown the same snowballs" as others around the stadium, will face their Creator after 120 years, and, like Cuddly Puppy, have nothing else to say but — *"I didn't know you would catch me."*

Amnesia

GIVING

The brave pioneer regained consciousness and slowly became aware of what had happened to him. Soon after he had arrived at his destination, a huge branch fell from a tree. It grazed his skull and rendered him senseless.

He was happy to be alive. But the accident affected his memory. "Why did my ruler send me to this distant place?" the pioneer wondered as he looked around.

There was much to behold. There was a great abundance of produce. The fruits were ripening; the vegetation was in full bloom.

"I was sent here," he reasoned, "to gather produce and to bring it home."

Which he did.

Back home, he stood before his ruler, proud of what he had done. The ruler, however, was less than pleased. "You obviously forgot why I sent you. The land you visited is indeed a land of great plenty. But it is also a land of great need. The natives are in great difficulty. They are suffering. I sent you there to teach them and to help them.

"You, however, apparently forgot this. You saw the wealth of the land, and you came to a different conclusion. That conclusion was incorrect.

"I sent you there to give. Yet, all you did was take."

Each of us is that pioneer. The distant land is this world. And our ruler is G-d.

At times, we forget why we were sent here. We lose sight of our mission. We believe that we are here to take. We forget that we are here to give.

The Torah (*Devarim* 8:7,9) states:

> *For Hashem, your G-d, is bringing you to a land that is good; a land of flowing rivers … a land in which nothing is missing.*

It then continues (8:11):

> *Be careful, lest you forget Hashem, your G-d.*

Amidst all the material things around us, and amidst the heavy emphasis placed on acquiring them, we can easily forget why we are here.

The great sage Hillel states (*Avot* 1:14):

> *"If I am only for myself, what am I?"*

If all of our actions center upon ourselves – if they center upon personal gain, materialism, and the feeding of our egos – then we have not fulfilled our missions in this world. If we are only "for ourselves," we are nothing.

∽∽

We live in a world that often overlooks people's obligations to each other. A recent personal experience illustrates this thought.

We were seeking photographs for a book about *chesed* (acts of kindness). Our graphic artist made us aware of a service available by computer. One simply enters in a key word, and photographs which represent that theme appear.

The artist entered the word *kindness*. The result? *No photographs appeared!*

Is that not symbolic of the world we live in? Without question, that world is often self-serving and selfish. What's "kindness"? There is far greater emphasis upon personal gain and selfish needs than there is upon helping others.

Is this good enough for us?

After all, we are here to observe the Torah and follow the *mitzvot*. And a substantial portion of those *mitzvot* are commandments that implore us to remember, in effect: *If I am only for myself, what am I?*

Let us learn from the Creator's first recorded instructions to Abraham, our forefather (*Bereishit* 12:1):

"Go forth from your land and from your birthplace."

Throughout the life of every Jew, he or she is compelled to exercise a personal *going forth (lech lecha)*. We must learn to *go out,* rise above the culture around us, and live by a higher standard.

If I am only for myself, what am I?

After all, without *chesed*, without kindness, the world cannot survive. Why not? Because we are interdependent. *We need each other*. You may have what somebody else needs. And somebody may have what you need.

We learn this from an incident in the Torah:

As the servant of Abraham was seeking a wife for Isaac, he prayed to the Creator to do *chesed* (an act of kindness) to his master, Abraham. He said (*Bereishit* 24:12):

> *"Hashem, the G-d of my master, Abraham, be with me today, and do chesed to my master, Abraham."*

The *Midrash* (*Bereishit Rabbah* 60) comments:

> *Rabbi Chaggai, in the name of Rabbi Yitzchak, said, "Everybody needs chesed, even Abraham."*

In a similar fashion, the *Pardes Yoseph* comments on the blessing *Borei Nefashot* (recited after eating certain foods). In that blessing, we praise G-d for creating many souls and "*chesronan*" – what they are lacking. He notes that everybody is lacking *something*. It is critical, therefore, that people help each other, since each of us has what somebody else needs.

After all, one person may have intelligence, but have financial difficulty. Another may be well-off financially, but have a health problem. A third person may be healthy, but have difficulty in "marrying off" a child. And so forth.

People need people.

Realizing this, we must ask ourselves:

- How much time do I spend helping others?
- Do I realize that I have something that somebody else needs?
- Do I spend too much of my time accumulating wealth, thinking of myself, and seeking pleasure?

Like the brave pioneer,
Have I forgotten what my mission is?

9 to 5

DEDICATION

Some experiences in life are expected to be stressful. Others are expected to be more peaceful, such as a routine visit to a quiet country store.*

On a recent day, I made such a visit. I was seeking to make some purchases.

I entered the store at approximately seven minutes to 5. Looking at the posted hours, I realized that the store would close at 5 o'clock. But seven minutes is a long time, and I felt confident that I could purchase what I wanted to.

A couple of minutes later, an announcement was made: "We are closing in five minutes. Please make your purchase now."

This was reasonable enough.

Soon a clerk approached me. "Sir, we are closing in three minutes." I began to feel a bit tense, and hurried to find the items I was seeking. The pressure was on.

*Some of the details in the following incident were intentionally altered in order to conceal the identity of the establishment in question. Also, times are approximate.

Then another announcement came, and it was very final: "The store is closed."

I had not found everything that I wanted, and, perhaps, hoped against hope that I could have a few more minutes. But it was not to be. I looked up, and saw all three or four sales-people – belongings in hand and fully ready to leave the premises – looking at me.

One said, pointing to a side door, "You can exit this way."

I left the store, entered my car, and looked at the clock. It was two minutes past the hour (with the two minutes being the amount of time it took me to reach my car).

In other words, the store closed *at exactly 5 o'clock*.

The "9-to-5" mentality dictates:

- *Work only as hard as you have to – and no more*.
- *Put in no extra time, no extra effort. The minimum is good enough*.

Unfortunately, many people approach their Jewish observance in exactly the same fashion. Yes, they follow the *mitzvot*. Yes, they are fully aware of their obligations. But they limit their actions to what *must* be done. They will do the minimum – and no more.
They are "9-to-5" Jews.

The Passover Sacrifice carried with it a number of specific laws. Among those statutes was the requirement that the individual who brings the sacrifice must be in a state of purity. He could not be impure (a status that results from coming into contact with a dead body). What if he was? What if he had been involved in burying the dead and became impure? Well, in that case, he is exempt from the obligation. He need not bring a sacrifice that year.

In the desert (during the forty-year period after the exodus from Egypt) a number of people approached Moses. These individuals had become impure – perhaps in the noble act of burying the dead. As mentioned, they were exempt from bringing the Passover Sacrifice.

However, they were not happy with this exemption. They asked (*Bamidbar* 9:7):

> *"Why should we lose out? Why should we not be able to bring the sacrifice of G-d in its time among the Children of Israel?"*

This is quite interesting. These people would have been exempt! They were fully within their rights, and could not have been faulted if they did not bring the sacrifice. *They had no obligation.* However, they had a love of *mitzvot*. And even if they had no obligation, they sought to do the *mitzvah* anyway. "Why," they asked, "should we lose out?"

As a consequence of their request, the directive came from the Creator, through Moses: *If somebody is impure at the pre-*

scribed time of this sacrifice, he may bring the sacrifice a month later.

To the person who loves *mitzvot*, simply doing what he or she is obligated to do is not satisfactory. Rather, such an individual *goes out of his or her way* to find *mitzvot* – to be proactive – and does not simply wait for the *mitzvot* to come.

After all, *why lose out?*

We must realize the following: Among the *mitzvot* – the commandments – there are *don'ts* and there are *do's.*

The *don'ts* are actions that we are prohibited from doing: lighting a fire on *Shabbat*, stealing, eating food that is not kosher.

The *do's* are *mitzvot* that we *must* do: saying *Shema* twice a day, eating matzah on Passover, and so forth.

However, even among the *do's*, there are two types of *mitzvot*: those which are linked to time, and those that are not.

The *mitzvot* that are linked to time have deadlines. You cannot, for example, let a quarter of the day go by without saying *Shema*. You cannot let the first night of Passover go by without eating matzah. And so forth.

The *mitzvot* that are not linked to time, however, have no deadlines: You could help the poor today, or you could not do so until tomorrow. You could visit somebody who is sick, today, or you could wait until tomorrow – or even until next year. You have no obligation to do these *mitzvot* on any given time schedule.

If you're not proactive, these *mitzvot* will not get done.

Consequently, the "9-to-5 Jew" – the individual who is satisfied to do only what he or she is obligated to do, and no more – lets these *mitzvot* go. "They are not a must for me *today*, so why do them?"

The proactive Jew, on the other hand, *looks for mitzvot to do*. This person goes out of his or her way to find *mitzvot*. Simply fulfilling obligations is not enough. He or she wants to do as many *mitzvot* as possible.

Do *you* wait for *mitzvot* to come to you? Or do you go after them?

For a change:

- Don't wait to be approached before giving a financial contribution. Discover a need, and take the initiative without being asked.
- Don't help others only after they ask you. Instead, offer the help on your own.
- Tell your children how you feel about them. Don't wait until they hint that they would like to know.
- Tell your parents how you feel about them. Don't wait until they hint that they would like to know.
- Tell your husband, your wife, how you feel. Don't wait until he or she hints that he or she would like to know.

- Be proactive in your Torah study. It's not enough to simply join a class that is taking place before or after prayers. Go out and find – even organize – a class or learning-session on the subject you would like to learn.
- Take a good look at your community. See what needs to be done. Take it upon yourself to make things better. Make it happen.
- Learn to open your eyes and ears to the needs of others. When you enter a crowded room, don't think only about yourself *(What do I look like? What do they think of me?)*. Instead, look around the room and ask yourself: *What can I do for others? Who needs help? Who needs encouragement? Who is lonely?*
- Look at your family and its dynamics. Is there room for improvement? Some people only awaken after there is a problem. Don't be one of them.

Wake up. Look around. Be aware.

In other words, be proactive. Don't sit back and wait for the *mitzvot* to come to you. Rather, go after them yourself. Why lose out? Go beyond, do *more* than you have to.

Don't be a 9-to-5 Jew.

G-d Knows That I Am Right

MAINTAINING A HIGHER STANDARD

What is your opinion of the following statement? *People may think that I am doing the wrong thing. But it doesn't matter. G-d knows that I am right.*

Is it enough to do what is good in the eyes of G-d? If we are doing the right thing, and people misunderstand, are we responsible?

∞∞

The *Midrash* (*Tanchuma, Vayechi,* 17) tells of the following:

Joseph and his brothers returned to Canaan, from Egypt, to bury their father Jacob. On the way back, Joseph left the group to make a highly personal detour – he visited the pit into which, years ago, he had been thrown by his brothers.

Much had happened to Joseph in the four decades since that incident took place. After being pulled from the pit in order to be sold into slavery, Joseph rose to a position of authority in Egypt. He therefore visited the pit to thank G-d for saving him.

The *Midrash* notes: His intentions were sincere *(leshem Shamayim)*.

The brothers, however, misunderstood. To them, Joseph was reminding himself of what his brothers had done to him at that site. Now, with their father deceased, Joseph would, *no doubt*, repay his brothers for their actions.

They said (*Bereishit* 50:15):

> *"Now, Joseph may hate us – and do to us in turn what we did to him."*

Of course, Joseph, once aware of this, put his brothers at ease, and explained that he bore no grudge.

However, we must ask the question: *Was it Joseph's responsibility to avoid doing something that his brothers might misunderstand? Or was it enough for him to say, in effect, "G-d knows that I am right"?*

The *Midrash* (*Mishnat Rabbi Eliezer*, 94) quotes the Torah (*Bamidbar* 32:22):

> *You must be clean in the eyes of G-d and in the eyes of the people of Israel.*

It *was* Joseph's responsibility to consider the feelings of his brothers, and avoid the ill will that a misunderstanding could bring. This holds true even though he was doing nothing wrong, and was acting *leshem Shamayim* – for sincere reasons.

Yes, you must consider what people think.

❧

The *Chatam Sofer* struggles with this concept in one of his *Responsa* (*Likkutim* 6:59). In a remarkably personal and moving statement, he writes:

All my days I have been pained by this statement [that one must be clean in the eyes of G-d and in the eyes of people] … it is more plausible to fulfill the first obligation, that is, the requirements of Heaven, than to fulfill the obligations of others … because people have strange thoughts.

Who knows what "strange thoughts" people have? Who knows what far-out suspicions are in people's minds? Still, they must be considered.

Where, we may ask, did the phrase, *"You must be clean in the eyes of G-d and the eyes of the people of Israel,"* originate?

Toward the end of the journey of the Jewish people in the desert, they conquered territory from the Amorite nation. Since this land was well suited to cattle, the tribes Gad and Reuven requested to stay there. Rather than cross into Canaan, the future Land of Israel, they would stay where they were.

Moses, after hearing the request, admonished them. He explained that the request could easily be construed in a negative manner. The other tribes might think that it was a reflection of fear, a reluctance to fight against the powerful people of Canaan.

The tribes then made a modified request: They would enter Canaan and fight alongside their brethren. Only after the Land was conquered would they return to occupy the land they were in.

In principle, Moses accepted their request. However, he added (*Bamidbar* 32:22):

> *"You must be clean in the eyes of G-d and in the eyes of the people of Israel."*

Even if G-d knew that their thoughts were good, they must not do something that would be misunderstood by others.

This message is conveyed, as well, by the extraordinary steps taken by a certain family. This family, known as Beit Avtinas, was in charge of preparing the *Ketoret* (the mixture of spices offered in the *Beit HaMikdash*, the Holy Temple, twice daily).

This family took upon itself a very strict prohibition: *Women from this family would never wear perfume.* In fact, even a girl who married into the family was asked to agree never to wear perfume. Why? So nobody would ever accuse them of using the *Ketoret* for personal purposes.

You must be clean in the eyes of G-d and in the eyes of the people of Israel.

Now, this family could have said otherwise. They could have said, "We are honest. We know it, and G-d knows it. Do we have to worry about people who accuse us without reason?"

Their answer is, in effect: "Yes!"

Here are further examples (*Yoreh Deah* 257:1) of the same concept:

- Somebody who collects money for charity, when counting that money in front of others, may not count two bills at one time. Why not? Because people may say: He will keep every second bill for himself.

- Additionally, somebody who normally collects money for charity may not take money which is owed to him personally and place it in his pocket. Why not? After all, it is his own money! Because somebody might think that the money is public money, not his own.

Now, let us ask: Why this concern for "what people think"? Why must we, as Jews, who have learned to be so independent minded, give any thought to the misconceptions of others?

First, we may answer, some of the above cases involve suspicion of leaders. Critical to our traditions and to our institutions is the confidence of our people in their leaders.

However, there is more to it.

We must realize that Judaism places great emphasis on people interacting with people. Many of our commandments promote closeness between people. Many discourage friction and dislike. *The Torah wants people to get along.*

When people suspect others, a barrier is erected between them. It just is not the same as it had been before.

True, we are obligated to give others the benefit of the doubt – and, therefore, have the right to expect that others will do the same with us. Why should we worry about their suspicions if those suspicions are contrary to our Jewish values? Because people are what they are, and not everybody has, to date, reached the level that he or she should be on. So suspicion exists, even though it is something that should not be.

Therefore, for the sake of closeness between people, we may not ignore the feelings, the "strange thoughts," as the *Chatam Sofer* calls them, of others. We must work on making friends and work on keeping friends – despite their frailties, foibles, and failings. We *do* have to concern ourselves with "what people think."

Yes, G-d knows when you are right. However, it is important that the people He created know this as well.

Procrastinators

DILIGENCE

The middle-aged man and his wife were sifting through memorabilia in their attic. They found old phonograph records, book reports, out-of-style clothing, and a receipt for dry cleaning. They examined the ticket: *Sam's Dry Cleaners. One pair of pants. April 3, 1962.*

Said the man to his wife, "Let's have some fun. *Let's go there*. I wonder if he's still in business."

The couple went to the location which was printed on the ticket. Indeed, the store was still in business. Same store, same location.

"I have an idea," said the man to his wife. "Let's go inside. We'll present the ticket, and see what happens."

Inside they went. And there was Sam, behind the counter: short man, gray hair, quite serious.

The man handed Sam the ticket. "Just one minute," replied Sam. He walked to the rear of the store, and returned two minutes later.

"I'm sorry," he said, "it's not ready yet. But I can have it for you Tuesday."

∞∞

Sam is the prototypical procrastinator. His thinking: *Why do something today, when you could put it off until tomorrow?*

Procrastinators coast through life, postponing change, and delaying self-improvement.

The Jewish version sounds something like this:

- *Study, attend a class? Sure. I'll begin next week.*
- *Improve Shabbat observance? Good idea. I'll start soon.*
- *Brush up on the laws of family purity? I'm all for it. Give me a few days.*
- *Devote more time to my children? A must! Any day now, I'll begin.*

In most cases, of course, the delay just continues. Procrastination is forever.

Poignant, then, is the statement of our Sages (*Mechilta*):

> *When a mitzvah comes into your hand, do not let it pass.*

Similarly, in *Parashat Vayakhel* (*Shemot* 35:10), the Torah states, regarding the need for people to construct the *Mishkan* (Tabernacle):

And all people, wise of heart, among you, should come and do everything that G-d commanded.

In a commentary on this *(HaDerush VeHaIyun),* it is stated:

Hesitating to do a mitzvah, and speaking about it, are prone to give rise to various obstacles, which will prevent fulfilling the mitzvah. For this reason, the Torah stated [in the sentence quoted above]: "And all people, wise of heart … should come and do … " — since one who is truly wise, and really wants to fulfill the commandments of the Creator, should not speak too much [before doing the mitzvah], or hesitate. Rather, he should come and do, immediately, with diligence.

Procrastination does not always sound irrational. In fact, it could often sound very convincing.

A woman visited her good friend, who had just moved to a new apartment.

"It's lovely!" she exclaimed. "But why don't you unpack? Why are you living out of your suitcase?"

"Oh," said the new resident, "I'm waiting until next week, when the walls will be painted."

Week Two, and another visit. "The walls are painted now. Why haven't you unpacked your suitcase?"

"Oh, I've decided to wait another week, until after the carpet is installed."

Week Three: Walls painted, carpet installed, clothing still in suitcase. "But you said you would —"

"I know. But next week they're going to ..."

And so on, forever.

Sound rational? Possibly. However, one who waits until everything is perfect before taking action will possibly be waiting for quite a while.

The Sage Hillel expressed it (*Avot* 2:4) this way:

"Do not say, 'When I have free time, I will study' – since you may never have free time."

Other examples:

I'd love to study, to attend classes. I'd love to improve my prayer, my berachot, my Shabbat. And I fully intend to do so, after (choose one):

- *I graduate;*
- *I get married;*
- *My child is born;*
- *My business runs smoothly;*
- *I move into my own home;*
- *My daughter gets married;*
- *My grandson has his bar mitzvah.*

The list of excuses is a virtual catalogue of life's milestones. And they could be quite convincing.

If we wait until all of life's bumps have disappeared, we may have quite a delay. If we put off doing good things until our minds are settled, we may in effect put them off forever. And if we procrastinate until things are perfect, we may never unpack our suitcases.

Let us not put off our mitzvot. Unlike Sam, we need not wait until Tuesday.

Sale!

TESHUVAH: A UNIQUE OPPORTUNITY

There appears to be a new national pastime: attending sales. Each week, bargain-hunting fanatics follow an identical routine. First, they scan local newspapers, carefully taking note of the locations of such events. Next, they hurry to the sites to compare their contents. Then, they return to the stores with the best values, to make their purchases. No opportunity is allowed to pass.

Well, smart shoppers, here's important news: The Jewish Calendar announces its *"annual sale."*

❦

In *Yeshayahu* (55:6) it states:

Seek G-d when He is there.

The *Gemara* (*Rosh Hashanah* 18a) notes:

This refers to the Ten Days of Teshuvah (repentance) from Rosh Hashanah through Yom Kippur.

Maimonides (*Laws of Teshuvah* 2:6) writes, regarding this:

Even though repentance and prayer are always effective, during the Ten Days, from Rosh Hashanah through Yom Kippur, they are even more effective, and accepted immediately, as is written, "Seek G-d when He is there."

We have, consequently, a unique opportunity for *teshuvah* (repentance). This is, in effect, an annual, ten-day "sale."

The very existence of *teshuvah* is a wonder. The *Gemara (Yerushalmi, Makkot* 2:6) relates:

Wisdom was asked: "What should be the fate of the sinner?" It answered: "He should be punished."

The Creator was asked: "What should be the fate of the sinner?" He answered: "Let him do teshuvah, and he will be forgiven."

This underlines an important thought. According to wisdom, according to logic, according to justice – *teshuvah* should not exist. After all, could we expect an action that was already done to be, in effect, erased, just because we said some words and thought some thoughts?

Well, this indeed is the case. *Teshuvah* does indeed exist, and it is available to us at all times. As noted in the excerpt from Maimonides, *teshuvah* is always effective and always available. It is not limited to one time of the year.

Consider this: According to the mystical teachings of the Kabbalah, the soul attempts to ascend to the Heavens every evening, as a person sleeps. If the soul has flaws, resulting from sins, it cannot ascend. We therefore say *Shema Yisrael* before sleeping, and recite a prayer of *teshuvah*, to purify ourselves.

Is there a practical side to this mystical concept? Yes, as follows: Evaluate your actions every evening. Seek to improve, to evaluate your conduct, to grow. You did something you regret? Avail yourself of the gift of *teshuvah*. Regret the action, acknowledge that it was done, and resolve to do better in the future.

Purify your soul.

After all, none of us is perfect. We must strive, daily, to progress, to advance, to bring holiness into our own lives and into the lives of our family members.

This can be done year-round. For ten days, however, it can be done more easily. Our prayers, our supplications and our *teshuvah* are more potent. They are accepted more readily.

Additionally, there is a one-month period prior to these ten days, which serves a vital purpose. This is the month of *Elul*. During this month, we must intensely search our souls, evaluate our deeds of the past year, pray for forgiveness, and develop plans for self-improvement.

Take this seriously. Perhaps make a list of your errors, your resolutions, your goals, and your plans. During the year, consult the list. Evaluate your progress.

Each of us should ask:

- How did I do during the past year?
- Which *mitzvot* should I add to the *mitzvot* I follow now?
- Which misdeeds should be eliminated from my lifestyle? And:
- Am I a better person, a better Jew, today, than I was one year ago?

Now we can enter the Ten Days of *Teshuvah* fully prepared, and ready to take full advantage of the opportunity afforded to us.

That opportunity must be taken. Its potential is infinite. No smart shopper should let it pass.

Crocodile Tears

"PULLING" FOR OTHERS

Sometimes, when a crocodile kills his prey, a fluid is secreted from its eyes. This fluid appears to be tears – but it is not. Though the prey may have been dismembered, limb by limb, what appears to be a feeling of sadness on the part of the crocodile is nothing of the kind.

The crocodile-tear phenomenon is not limited to reptiles. It can be found in one species of mammal as well – though in a less violent fashion. Lest you fear that you have stumbled upon an article on animal biology, we will identify the mammal in question. It is known as the *human being*.

Humans know that there are times in which they are *expected* to feel bad. If a friend or acquaintance suffers a financial setback, for example, one is *expected* to be unhappy. Due to envy, however, this often is not the case. Sure, it appears that the friend is deeply saddened. In reality, however, the false expressions of sadness are nothing more than *crocodile tears*.

Envy – the state of mind prohibited by our tenth commandment – does this to people. It causes them, at best, to be immune to a setback of a friend. And it causes them, at worst, to *hope* for it. Envious people do not "pull" *for* their friends. They pull *against* them.

☙❧

Perhaps the prototype of envy – for the ages – is portrayed in a well-known incident in the life of King Solomon (*Melachim Aleph* 3:16-27):

> *Then two women came before the king.*

One claimed that the baby which had died belonged to her friend, while the baby that was alive belonged to her. The other woman made the identical claim regarding herself: The dead baby belonged to her friend, while the living baby was hers.

Both claimed:

> *"My son is the living one and your son is dead."*

As is well known,

> *The king replied,"Bring me a sword." And they brought the sword before the king. And the king said, "Cut the living child in two, and give half to one and half to the other."*

Let us note closely what each of the two women said at this point:

The real mother said:

> *"Please, my master, give her the living child. Do not kill him."*

The other woman said:

> *"Let it not be mine, let it not be yours. Cut it."*

How can we explain the strange reaction of the false mother? What would she gain if the baby were killed?

The answer: *In reality, nothing.* However, that is the nature of envy. It does not matter if one does not have something. *As long as nobody else has it.*

Again: Envious people do not pull *for* their friends. They pull *against* them.

∽∼

A story comes to mind. It is based on a true incident, but certain details have been changed to protect the identities of the people involved.

Two families – they were cousins, in fact – were envious of each other. Each family sought to outdo the other. They were in constant competition.

Suddenly, one day, one of the families received startling news: *Their cousins had won a huge sum of money in the lottery!*

How did they feel about their cousins' sudden windfall? They were "sick" about it! The mother of the wounded family made a valiant effort to help her children adjust to what had happened. She said to them, "Maybe it isn't true!"

Once again: Envious people do not pull *for* their friends. They pull *against* them.

Is this how we want to be? Is this how we are to react to the successes of family and friends? Is there no way that we can accept somebody being more successful than we are?

After all, in *Mishlei* (24:17) we learn:

> *When your enemy falls, do not rejoice.*

Understandably, one must be taught to control the temptation to rejoice when an *enemy* falls. Need we also be told not to rejoice when a *friend* falls?

There must be some way that we can teach ourselves to cry *real* tears – not the crocodile type – when our friends are in pain; and to rejoice – *sincerely* – when our friends prosper. There must be some way that we can control – or, better yet, eliminate – the envy that we know we should not have.

There is — by understanding a few critical ideas:

(1) *A state of affairs is "win-win" when an action brings with it not one, but, rather, two positives.*

Regarding a person who gives, we learn (*Tehillim* 37:26):

Every day, he has mercy upon others. He lends to them. As a result, his offspring are blessed.

How are the offspring – the children of this giving, kind person – blessed? They are blessed in two ways:

- As a reward for the parent's deeds, there is a special blessing to the children from the Creator.
- As a natural consequence of the parent's deeds, the children become better people.

The *giving* home is "win-win."

(2) *Whatever we have is given to us by the Creator.*

Rabbi Abraham ibn Ezra, in his commentary on the tenth commandment, *"Do not envy"* (*Shemot* 20:14), notes:

Many people have wondered: How can one control what comes into his or her mind? How could we possibly observe this commandment?

He answers:

[Things that are desirable] do not come to a person because of his wisdom or his knowledge. Rather, it depends upon what the Creator gives him.

Ibn Ezra quotes from *Kohelet* (2:21):

There may be a man who works with wisdom, knowledge, and talent. Yet his portion is given to a man who did not work for it.

Ibn Ezra also notes that our Sages stated (*Moed Katan* 28a):

> *The number of children that a person has, the length of a person's life, and a person's income do not depend on merits.*

Some things are beyond your control. If you don't have something, it may be because the Creator does not want you to. He knows what is good for you and what is not. He knows what you need and do not need.

(3) *Avoid being obsessed with the things you are missing, and focus on the things you have.*

Our Sages make a comparison of words used in two incidents which occurred thousands of years apart. The first source is the story of Adam and Eve, in which the words *"hamin ha'eitz,"* referring to the Tree of Knowledge, are used (*Bereishit* 3:11):

> *"Have you eaten of the tree from which I commanded you not to eat?"*

The second source is the Purim story of *Megillat Esther*, in which the words *"Haman"* and *"ha'eitz* (the tree)*"* occur in close proximity (*Megillat Esther* 7:10):

> *And they hanged Haman from the tree.*

The Hebrew letters of these two sets of words are the same. But other than the words, is there another comparison that can be made between these events?

Our Sages tell us that there is.

Adam was allowed to eat from any tree of the garden, with the exception of one. Yet he could not bear it. He had to eat from that tree.

By the same token, Haman had virtually everything he could want. He had wealth, honor, and respect. Everybody bowed to him – except one solitary Jew named Mordechai. Yet Haman could not bear this. Despite all he had, this, too, he wanted as well.

To some extent, we are the same way. We may have practically everything, That, however, is not good enough. We become obsessed with what we *do not* have. We must have it all.

Are we not much like Adam? Are we any less irrational than Haman?

∞∞

Let us all work on controlling envy. Let us pull *for* our friends, not *against* them. Let us rejoice when friends succeed. Let us be saddened when they do not. Let us have real feelings for others, not false feelings or *crocodile tears*.

White Elephants

AVOIDING DESPERATION

The king of an ancient oriental kingdom was fond of giving presents to selected individuals. Among his favored gifts were white elephants.

Though the creatures were rare, receiving one was anything but a blessing. The cost of feeding and lodging this huge mammal was staggering, and could easily bankrupt the "lucky" beneficiary.

To this day, a gift that brings more harm than good is appropriately called *a white elephant*.

As we navigate through life, many opportunities cross our paths. Some will indeed enhance our lives. Others *appear* to be good, but are not. When one is desperate, however, the choice becomes even more difficult. People are then even more likely to welcome a white elephant into their lives, and more prone to overlook the dangers it has in store.

A biblical case-in-point is the Korach-led challenge to the authority of Moses (*Bamidbar,* Ch. 16):

> *And Korach, the son of Yitzhar, who was the son of Kehat, who was the son of Levi; and Datan and Aviram, children of Eliav; and On the son of Pelet of the tribe of Reuven took themselves aside. And they took issue with Moses and Aaron.*

This incident raises many questions: How could an insurgency against a beloved leader receive any support among his people? How could *any* Jew, after witnessing nothing less than ten plagues, the splitting of the sea, and the revelation at Mount Sinai any Jew who was nourished by miracle upon miracle during the lifetime of Moses – be taken in by the transparent, self-serving designs of Korach?

According to *Ramban*:

> *This incident occurred in the desert of Paran. Before this, the people had loved Moses as they loved themselves. And, if any person had challenged Moses, the people would have stoned that person. Once, however, they had come to the desert of Paran ... and once it was decreed by G-d that they would die in the desert and never enter into the land of Israel – then the spirit of the people was bitter, and then Korach found an opening to question the authority of Moses.*

Again: *The spirit of the people was bitter*.

They were discouraged. They were dejected. *They were desperate*.

Did Korach provide something that would indeed improve the lot of the Jewish people? Was the alternative that he offered something of real promise? Of course not. Those who joined his rebellion soon joined him in ruin.

Korach's gift to those who followed him was no gift at all. It was, instead, *a white elephant*.

So it is in life. When a person is down and out, he or she is vulnerable. An offer which promises progress, improvement, and a better life is difficult to refuse. Yet, frequently, these offers produce no positive result, and, to the contrary, lead the recipient down the path to ruin.

We present two scenarios:

(1) The *financial* white elephant:

Ben's economic life is in turmoil. His personal expenses cannot be met; his creditors are unrelenting; and every ring of the telephone sends shivers down his spine.

Jacob, a friend, enters the picture. Jacob's own financial history is far from a success story. There was always great optimism, but there was always little success.

Jacob now invites Ben to join him in his latest venture. "We'll be partners, fifty-fifty. Of course, you'll have to invest some money, and I know it might take a second mortgage on your home to acquire it. But this is a unique opportunity."

Ben accepts the offer, and finds that it is indeed unique – uniquely suited to driving him deeper into debt, and motivating his bank to foreclose on his home.

(2) The *social* white elephant:

Sarah is getting older. Most of her friends are married. And not much is happening socially.

Enter the "White Knight," the young man who has everything: looks, financial security — and an addiction to gambling. "But," he insists, "don't worry! I haven't gambled in months! That trip to Atlantic City last week was for business."

Sarah marries him. And her worst fears are confirmed. His gambling addiction, it turns out, had never ceased. And the marriage ends in divorce.

The "White Knight" was actually a white elephant.

Incidentally, Sarah's story occurs in a number of variations. Instead of a gambling problem, we could substitute a drug problem, alcohol addiction, or an ethics problem. Regardless of which weakness the prospective mate has, the scenario is real and it is common. The Sarahs of the world, feeling desperate, overlook dangers and see only good.

Let us examine this message more closely. Are we contending that, no matter how down and out a person is, he or she should always take the most conservative, safe approach?

Must this individual wait with superhuman patience until a perfect opportunity comes along?

Our answers: *no* and *no*. The conservative approach is not always the wisest. And one who waits for perfection may wait forever.

But —

When an individual feels desperate, he or she is not in the best position to make decisions. The temptation to take a risk – the enticement to instantly conquer all problems with one bold stroke – is often overwhelming.

Seek counsel from a parent, a rabbi, or an elder. Take advice from somebody who could take an objective look at your life – without the wishful thinking and false optimism that you, yourself, may exhibit.

Keep the following in mind: Desperation is a state of mind. The man, the woman, of *emunah* (faith) is supremely suited to deal with adversity. He or she is not crushed by difficulty. On the contrary – the adversity is seen as an opportunity for growth, as a test, as a challenge. And there is supreme belief in the power of prayer. There is no reason to make irrational moves, no reason to gamble, no reason to be desperate.

There is no reason to accept a white elephant.

Take a Dose of Emunah

OVERCOMING STRESS

For physical illness, there is medication. *Take two aspirin and see me in the morning.*

Is there a medication for stress? Is there a mental "medicine" to cure it? Better yet, is there something we can take *to prevent it?*

Yes, there is.

In 1989, a powerful earthquake shook Armenia. There was enormous loss of life. One man's experience in that event unfolded, more or less, in the following fashion:

The man had taken his young son to school that morning. Now, following the earthquake, he feared for the safety of that son. The father ran to the school, and was horrified by what mhe saw. The tremor had leveled the school. The building had collapsed.

The man thought of his son. He recalled tucking him into bed each evening, with the words, "No matter what, I'll always be there for you."

Now the father ran to the site where his son's classroom had been. There was a pile of debris. He began to dig, removing stone after stone. He asked for help from others, who refused. Nevertheless, the man continued to dig – through the night, through the rain. Twelve hours, twenty-four, thirty-six.

In the thirty-eighth hour, he heard a voice.

"Dad, is that you? The collapsed stones formed a wedge, which kept us safe. Dad, I told my friends that you would come for me, if you were alive. And I told them that when you saved me, you would save them, too. I knew that no matter what, you would be there for me."

Although the incident is a true story, it serves as a metaphor for our relationship with our Creator. We are the sons. We are the daughters. He is the Father. Our *emunah* (faith) teaches us to believe that *no matter what, He will always be there for us.*

Yes, there is medication to prevent stress: *Take a dose of emunah, and see me in the morning.*

☙❧

The man or the woman of faith has a built-in antidote to stress – the knowledge that there is a Higher Authority Who is watching us and protecting us.

In the desert, G-d stated to the people of Israel (*Shemot* 23:20):

> *"Behold, I am sending an angel to guard you upon the way."*

Regarding this, the *Midrash* (*Shemot Rabbah* 32) explains:
G-d said to Moses, *"He who guarded the forefathers will guard the children."*

And so we see with Abraham, in his words to his servant Eliezer, as he sent him to find a wife for Yitzchak (*Bereishit* 24:7):

> *"G-d, Who is the G-d of the Heavens ... will send His angel before you."*

The *Midrash* adds:

> *[Also] Jacob our forefather, what did he say to his sons? "The angel who saves me from all evil [Bereishit 48:16] ...saved me from Esau and saved me from Lavan...he nourished me and sustained me during the years of famine."*

Stress comes from many origins. Some of it is trivial – a traffic jam, an appliance which does not operate properly, and the like. But some stress comes from more serious sources –

worries about health, money, and finding a husband or wife.

We shall discuss each of the three.

First, let us discuss *health*.

Many an individual is under stress regarding health – either the person's own health, or that of a relative or friend. We counter with a story:

A rabbi received a phone call: "My brother was in a serious car accident. He's in a coma. And I don't know how to tell the news to my 80-year-old father."

The rabbi went to the home of the elderly man. "I'd like you to come with me for a while," he said. The man agreed, and the two rode to the hospital. On the way, the rabbi began to break the news. "Your son was in an accident," he said.

The elderly man replied, "With *Hashem's* help, he will be fine." He then proceeded to discuss a section of Talmud which he had been learning.

As they neared the hospital, the rabbi turned to the elderly father and revealed more. "I hear it was a bad accident."

There was no reply.

They reached the hospital and entered the son's room. The doctors had given the patient a few hours to live.

"Don't worry, he will be fine," said the old man.

The people who were present felt bad for the aged father. Perhaps he was senile. Maybe he was in denial.

Then the elderly man spoke, and explained. "When the *Chafetz Chaim* [one of the great Sages of this century] wrote

Mishnah Berurah [his classic commentary on *Shulchan Aruch*], he wanted to be certain that it was clear to the common man. So he asked a few of us to read from it, and make comments – which I did.

"A while later, I asked him for a blessing. He did bless me, saying, 'You will live a long life. And during your lifetime, none of your children will pass away.'

"I know, therefore, that my son will live."

The next day, the son moved his legs and opened his eyes. A few days later, he was released from the hospital.

The power of a blessing! And the power of prayer! Stand before your Creator. Give voice to the stirrings of your heart. Pray for health – for yourself, for others.

No matter what, He is always there for us.

For stress related to health and well-being, *take a dose of emunah, and see me in the morning.*

Let us now discuss the stress of money. The business, the house, the mortgage, the bills, the bills, the bills. However, the man or the woman of faith puts money and materialism in proper perspective: They are not what we were placed here to attain. They are not the cornerstones of life. They are not what we are about. And they are not worth the stress.

Another story:

Two men contended over a parcel of land. One said it was his, the other said it was his. The rabbi decided to "ask" the land for its answer. He bent down, and placed his ear upon the ground. Then he stood up and stated the following:

"The land said, 'It doesn't matter if it belongs to you, or if, rather, it belongs to you – because someday the two of you will belong to the land.' "

Don't be stressed about money. Do your work, earn a living, but don't overvalue material things. Let faith set the tone.

Take a dose of emunah, and see me in the morning.

We now turn to another source of stress – the search for a husband, the search for a wife.

"There's nobody out there for me," one may think. As a result, there is stress. Often, in addition to the stress, there is something else – a lowering of personal standards. The boy or the girl compromises beliefs, morality, and manner of dress – in order to attract, someway, somehow, a prospective mate. After all, "There's nobody out there for me."

Allow us to quote from the Talmud (*Sotah* 2a):

> *Rabbi Yehudah said in the name of Rav, "Forty days before a child is conceived, a voice proclaims: The daughter of _____ will marry _____ ."*

In other words, there is somebody designated for everyone. Sure, you must take the proper steps. Yes, you must take the opportunity when it arises. But there is somebody for everyone.

Under stress about getting married? The Creator, *no matter what*, is there for you.

Take a dose of emunah, and see me in the morning.

Step back for a moment, and think: What does it say about our faith, when we give up hope? What statement are we making about our belief, when we are filled with worry, anxiety, and stress? Where are our Jewish values, if we have constant worry?

Remember: No matter what, our Creator is there for us.

Yes, there is an antidote to stress:

Take a dose of emunah, and see me in the morning.

The Misery Task Force

APPRECIATING WHAT WE HAVE

As members of the Misery Task Force, you are all well aware of your mission: *to make lives miserable.*

Now, according to the rules under which you operate, *you may not make any changes in the lives of your intended victims*. You may not damage their health, their financial status, or any other dimension of their lives. All of this is off-limits. However, there are weapons which you have at your disposal. These weapons, actually, are concepts. Teaching these concepts to your clients will make them feel unhappy, dissatisfied, and deprived.

You must note that this may not be very easy. One of the forefathers of the Jewish people, Jacob, set a precedent which is contrary to everything the Misery Task Force stands for. He said to G-d (*Bereishit* 32:11):

> *"I am made small [humbled] by all the acts of kindness and all the truth which you have done with Your servant. For with [only] my rod I have crossed this Jordan [River], and now I have become two camps."*

Jacob compared what he had *before* to what he had *then*, and was overwhelmed.

Of course, attitudes such as this are contrary to everything our task force stands for. It is therefore incumbent upon you, as members of the task force, to stress the concepts which will promote unhappiness and misery.

There are three such concepts.

(1) *Only new things can make you happy.* Teach your clients to think that anything which they have always had could not possibly be enough to bring happiness. Happiness only comes from something that is new.

In *Chovot HaLevavot* (*Duties of the Heart*, by Rabbi Bachya ibn Pakuda), two people are compared. One is adopted at infancy by a philanthropist. He is raised to adulthood by this generous man. He is fed, clothed, and provided with all his needs. The other person is not as fortunate. He is imprisoned by an enemy for an extended period of time. He is deprived of food and treated with disdain.

After many years, the prisoner is freed, and placed in the care of the philanthropist, who provides him with food, clothing, and other necessities. However, he does all this to a lesser extent than for the child he adopted.

Which beneficiary is more content? The former prisoner, of course. Though he received less, he appreciated more. The food, the clothing, and the care had not always been there.

Consequently, they are appreciated. Had they *always* been there, they would not be.

It does not matter how much good your client has in his or her life. Whatever is not new can easily be taken for granted.

Here's a perfect example:

A New York real-estate developer, much of whose wealth had been inherited, filed for bankruptcy. In his request for a court-appointed allowance, he listed the operating expenses – the supposed necessities of life – which he required for a six-month period.

They were as follows:

- $74,034 in salaries for the crew of his yacht.
- $26,370 for insurance on his collection of vintage cars.
- $465,142 for staff salaries at his Long Island home.

One becomes accustomed to certain amenities – especially if he or she has always had them.

You must prevent your clients from reflecting upon all the good which they have. Do not let them appreciate their health, the limbs of their bodies, their senses, their families, their community. Teach them: Only *new* things should make you happy.

(2) *Compare yourselves to others.* Try to convince your clients to compare themselves to others. That way, it does not matter how much your clients have. As long as others have more, your clients will never be happy.

If they need role models, they can turn to ballplayers. One signs a contract for $10 million per year. He is overjoyed – until another ballplayer signs a contract for $11 million per year. Suddenly, the first player is unhappy. He even loses his incentive to play. We can't expect him to give his full effort for $10 million per year, could we?

As is the case in sports, so is the case in everyday life.

Mr. Average owns a home and a car. He feeds his family well and has enough money to pay his bills. However, Mr. Average made one mistake in life: *He moved next door to Mr. More-Than-Average.* This man owns a nicer home. He drives a better car. He feeds his family exquisitely. When Mr. Average looks toward the home next door, *he is miserable.*

If you can successfully teach your clients to compare themselves to others, you are guaranteed to make them unhappy.

(3) *Only expensive things can make you happy.*

We again cite *Duties of the Heart* (*Shaar HaBechinah*, Ch. 5): The Creator has provided mankind with the necessities of life *in proportion to the quantities in which they are needed.* Air, for example, is essential at all times, so it is everywhere. Food is also a necessity, though not to the extent of air. So food, too, is plentiful, but it is not as abundant as air. In contrast are such things as gold, silver, and diamonds. Their utility to man is much less than air and food. So they are provided in short supply.

How, then, does mankind react? We think: Air? It's all over the place. Nothing special. Food? Same. On the other hand: Diamonds? Gold? Silver? They're scarce. They're expensive. They're special!

To keep your clients miserable, you must encourage them to think like this. You must reinforce their notion that whatever is scarce is special, and whatever is plentiful cannot be that good.

In conclusion: Your clients' states of mind are in your hands. If you can teach them to focus on the negative, you can turn their happiness into sorrow. You can fill their lives with misery – even if they have everything to be thankful for.

Syndromania

SELF-CONFIDENCE

We propose to introduce a new word into the lexicon of the English language. The word is *syndromania*.

> **syndromania** (*sin-dro-may-nee-a*) n. **1:** the tendency to blame any failure or misdeed upon a syndrome or disorder. **2:** the propensity to set low expectations for an individual, based on a belief that he or she suffers from a syndrome or disorder, and has little or no control over personal actions.

Syndromania is everywhere. In Texas lawyers plead the case of a defendant accused of murder. Their defense: He was suffering from "urban survival syndrome." A Pennsylvania man is accused of murdering his wife. His defense: A "sleep disorder" led him to pick up the gun and pull the trigger.

To some thinkers, a syndrome, a disorder, or a handicap is cause enough, *in and of itself,* to bring failure in any arena of life. The individual who suffers from any such condition is not expected to accomplish much. Others expect to see little success and much failure from the individual. Consequently, he or she develops low personal expectations as well.

∞∞

Is it beyond the realm of possibility that the handicap can be overcome and success attained?

Consider, for a moment, the Biblical personality Joseph. His trials and tribulations are well documented in the Torah. He was despised by his brothers, sold into slavery, imprisoned on false charges, and forced to fend for himself in the land of Egypt.

Imagine, now, a typical assessment of his potential:

> *First Name:* Joseph
> *Last Name:* Unavailable
> *Age:* 30
> *Nationality:* Hebrew
> *Relevant data:* Has had no communication with family in recent years. Known to wear multicolored garment when young; garment now misplaced. Has fascination with dreams. Suffered through traumatic family episode at age 17.

Outlook:

- Undoubtedly has no strong moral convictions, due to the absence of a father figure during critical years in his youth.
- Likely suffers from insecurity and lack of confidence, due to the discrimination he endured in a foreign land.

- In all probability, was permanently scarred by intense sibling rivalry with his brothers.

The reality, of course, was quite the opposite:

No strong moral convictions? On the contrary! When tested by the wife of his master, who made advances toward him, he said (*Bereishit* 39:9):

> *"And how could I commit this evil act — it is a sin against God!"*

Insecurity? Lack of confidence? He had no reservations about advising even Pharaoh what to do (*Bereishit* 41:34-35):

> *"Pharaoh should set appointees over the land ... and they should gather all the food of good coming years."*

Sibling rivalry left permanent scars? To his brothers, who sold him into slavery, he said, forgivingly (*Bereishit* 45:8):

> *"You did not send me here, G-d did."*

Joseph overcame the obstacles. He succeeded. So can others.

The man or woman of *emunah* (faith) is undaunted by obstacles. As we state in our daily prayers, *"It is in your [G–d's] power to make great, to strengthen, anybody."*

Nobody is a certain failure: not the child of a foster home, a broken home, or any home. Not the victim of discrimination, abuse, or ridicule. Not the child raised in poverty. Not the physically handicapped. And not the individual suffering from any of the countless syndromes and disorders catalogued by contemporary social science.

On the other hand, nobody is guaranteed success: not the child of the best home, not the brilliant few, not the talented, and not the child of wealth.

Let's face it. We all know people who had every excuse in the world to fail – and made it. And, unfortunately, we all know people who had every advantage for success – and failed.

Are disorders and syndromes just products of social scientists' imaginations? Absolutely not. Are there valid reasons to identify a disorder and, further, treat it? Without a question. Does the individual who suffers from these conditions have limitations and obstacles which other people do not? Of course.

However, we must recall the following: Whenever we identify a handicap, we run the risk of lowering expectations – both the expectations of the individual who has the handicap, and the expectations of the people who interact with the person. Those people – teachers, employers, family members – often become unwitting accomplices in holding down the self-esteem of the person.

Yes, a disorder may be a handicap. Yes, the person who suffers from it has difficulty doing things that others can accomplish with ease. But far be it from us – their counselors, their teachers, their parents, their friends – to cause them to lose hope. Far be it from us to be swept up in *syndromania*.

Win-Win

DO MITZVOT, BENEFIT YOUR CHILDREN

The poor widow, realizing that her young son was ill, had no choice: She would be forced to go door-to-door to find something for him to eat. *He must have chicken soup*, she decided.

She knocked on a door. It happened to be the home of a rabbinical student, who had eight children. She asked, "Could you, by any chance, spare a chicken for *Shabbat*?"

Actually, the man had two chickens in his refrigerator. But this was just enough for his own family. "I'm sorry," he answered. "I can't."

"Please, sir, my son is ill."

The man felt her pain. But his own family was also in difficult straits. Again, politely, he refused.

The woman persisted. "Please help a widow."

The man reconsidered. "All right. Please come in and have a seat. I'll just be a minute."

The man walked into the kitchen. A few seconds later, there was a loud scream. *The man's 2-year-old son had been locked in the refrigerator!* By opening its door to perform the *mitzvah*, the man saved his son's life.

This is a tale of *win-win*. The man won by fulfilling the *mitzvah* of charity. And he won again in saving his child's life.

∞∞∞

The above incident is true, but it can also serve as a parable: The child represents all Jewish children. The man represents every Jewish parent. And the *mitzvah* of charity represents a lifestyle of Torah and *mitzvot*. When parents commit themselves to *mitzvot* and follow a Torah lifestyle, they win once by serving the Creator. And they win again by saving the lives of their children.

Saving the lives of their children? Yes. Saving them from a life without meaning. And, perhaps, saving them from a life of problems.

How do parents' commitment to *mitzvot* save a child's life?

In *Tehillim* 37:26, we are taught about the person who is sensitive to others:

> *Every day, he has mercy upon others. He lends to them. As a result, his offspring are blessed.*

How are the offspring – the children of this giving, kind person – blessed? They are blessed in two ways:

(1) As a *reward* for the parent's deeds, there is a special blessing to the children from G-d.

(2) As a *natural consequence* of the parent's deeds, the children become better people.

Incidentally, this is not a consequence only of the *mitzvah*
of charity. It is a consequence of all the *mitzvot*.

The blessing that comes as a reward for the parents' deeds
is self-explanatory. Let us discuss the second way in which the
offspring are blessed: as a natural consequence of the parents'
deeds. How does it work? How do the deeds of the parent naturally bless the child?

Well, first, the children will learn from their parents, and
follow in their good ways. They will naturally observe the
same *mitzvot*. This is a blessing.

Additionally, there is a second natural consequence of the
parents' *mitzvot*: A much more wholesome environment is
created for the children. After all, what chance does a child
have without this? What are the odds of a young person, void
of Torah, leading a meaningful life? What are the chances that
a young person leading a secular life will stay away from serious addictions, develop self-discipline, meet and choose a
proper mate in marriage, and have the strength of character
to be a good husband or wife?

Our opinion is that the chances are slim.

Parents should consider the following:

In *Parashat Shoftim* (*Devarim* 20:19) the Torah states:

> *If you lay siege to a city for many days to wage war against it, to capture it, do not destroy its trees by putting an axe to them – for it is from them you will eat.*

This is a prohibition upon destroying fruit trees in wartime. Why? Because once you conquer the city, you will need those trees for sustenance (*Rashbam* and *Sforno*).

From this, we can make a comparison to our commitment to *mitzvot*: If one eliminates *mitzvot* (the "trees") from his or her own life, and, as a consequence, eliminates them from the lives of the children, something has been destroyed that will have critical effects in the future. How important those *mitzvot* would have been for the children! Those "trees" that were cut down could have "nourished" them in the years ahead.

Every so often, on weekdays, I call people to join us for the morning *minyan*. Usually, these calls are made at about 6:30 a.m.

At one time, I was a bit reluctant to call someone at such an hour. Is it too early? Will I wake up his wife? Will he be upset?

Today, I have very little hesitation. The call might save his children. It might save his marriage. Who knows? By being part of a synagogue; by praying three times daily; by joining a class; by being around committed people, a man takes a giant step forward for his family.

Once, as I was retrieving my telephone messages in the synagogue, I received the following message, in a woman's voice that I recognized: "Call [her husband] to come to prayers, but don't tell him I told you."

This is one smart woman. Obviously, she recognizes the importance for her family.

Do anything you can to involve your family in Torah and *mitzvot*! Get them involved in a synagogue, get them to classes, let them be close to a rabbi, make sure they pray. *You might be saving their lives.*

Through a parent's involvement in *mitzvot*, his or her offspring are blessed. Nourish the trees of Torah – do not cut them down. Like the man in the story, you might save the lives of your children by doing *mitzvot*. You can't lose. On the contrary – *it's win-win.*

I Remain...

ENTHUSIASM

A certain familiar closing to letters seems to be without meaning, as follows:

Dear David,

> *I enjoyed our meeting. Let's keep in touch. Hope to see you soon.*

> *I remain,*
> *Abraham Cohen*

This has no meaning. Of course he *remains* Abraham Cohen. Did we think that he changed his name?

Actually, "I remain" should be followed by another phrase, such as "sincerely yours," "faithfully yours," or "your loyal servant." It thus becomes, "I remain sincerely yours," "I remain faithfully yours," or "I remain your loyal servant." These phrases indeed have meaning. All convey a similar message: The intensity of the writer's feelings has not changed.

A person may have strong feelings. Those feelings, however, may last only a brief time. If one can *maintain* those feelings – if one could honestly state *"I remain"* about those feelings – he or she will have conveyed a strong message of commitment.

This brings us to the emotion we call *enthusiasm*. Often, this emotion is marked by great intensity. This intensity, however, often wanes. *Generating* enthusiasm is not unusual. *Maintaining* it is quite rare. It is difficult to say, "*I remain* enthusiastically yours."

Our laws and traditions are, to us, beloved and cherished. We long for a life of *kedushah*, of holiness. Consequently, our feelings about Torah, about *mitzvot*, are quite strong.

But, as noted above, enthusiasm is an emotion which often does not last. Considering that most *mitzvot* which we perform are not at all new to us – in fact, many have been performed by us hundreds of times – maintaining a high level of intensity does not come easily.

Without real effort in this matter, our intensity weakens. We tend to carry out *mitzvot* mechanically. We go through the motions listlessly, with no feeling. There is no intensity. There is no emotion. Enthusiasm is missing in action.

Must it be this way?

Our patriarch, Abraham, did not think so. When the three "men" visited Abraham (*Bereishit* 18:2-7):

> *And he [Abraham] saw, and he ran to meet them … and Abraham hurried to the tent … and Abraham ran to the cattle, and he took a calf, tender and good … and he hurried to prepare it.*

A seemingly simple incident, but what a lesson! This could not have been the first time Abraham had guests. Undoubtedly, he had performed *hachnassat orchim*, inviting guests, hundreds of times before. Yet nothing was mechanical. Nothing was without feeling. He ran. He hurried. The enthusiasm was there.

We must teach ourselves to do this. Yes, it requires work. Yes, it requires effort. It is not, however, impossible. If our love of *mitzvot* is there, then intensity in performing them can, with some effort, be maintained.

Why is this important?

Mitzvot are more than pass-fail. One can perform a *mitzvah*, and technically fulfill his or her minimal obligation. One could, so to speak, *pass*. However, one could do vastly more in performing the very same *mitzvah* – by performing it with understanding, with feeling, with emotion.

For many an individual, this should be the next spiritual battleground. If you've already made a successful effort toward adding new *mitzvot*, now make an effort toward improving the old ones. You've added to the quantity. Now, improve the quality. Add *kedushah,* holiness, to your life. Add feeling. Add emotion. Add enthusiasm.

After all,

- One could pray with feeling — or pray without it.
- One could study with feeling — or study without it.
- One could observe *Shabbat* with feeling — or without.
- One could help others, financially or otherwise, with feeling — or without.

How vastly more meaningful and more rewarding are our *mitzvot* when performed with the intensity and feeling that our love for them deserves!

Let us each sit down, and write an imaginary letter to our Creator:

Dear G-d,

Your mitzvot are very beloved to me. I am making every effort to perform them. Even when there is a mitzvah which I have carried out many times before, I make every effort to perform it properly – with feeling, with intensity, with emotion.

I remain enthusiastically yours,
[Your Name Here]

Litmus Test

PERFORMING UNDER STRESS

If you learned anything at all in chemistry class, you learned about *litmus paper.*

Testing for the presence of an acid? Immerse blue litmus paper into a solution. If the liquid is an acid, the paper will turn red. Testing for the presence of a base? Immerse red litmus paper into a solution. If the liquid is a base, the paper will turn blue.

Question: Is there a *litmus test* of a person's character?

Answer: Yes. In the *Gemara* (*Eruvin* 65b) it is stated:

> *A person is recognized by three measures – his cup, his pocket, and his anger (bekosso, bekisso, beka'aso).*

What do these three have in common? *They all represent moments of stress.*

- *His cup.* After drinking, a person's self-control is weakened. Can he maintain his standards – despite his condition?

- *His pocket*. How does he or she act in financial matters? For many, this is the *ultimate* test. If you can't make ends meet, do you abandon Torah guidelines? Do you close your eyes to the ethics which the *mitzvot* mandate? Or do you stand strong?
- *His anger*. You were embarrassed. Slighted. Overlooked. Ignored. Forgotten. Your blood comes slowly to a boil, then simmers. Will words leave your tongue which should not be said? Will you embarrass, slight, overlook, ignore, forget – in return? Will your words take on a life of their own? Or will you hold them in check, and maintain your self-discipline?

The litmus test represented by the above three character dimensions may be simply summarized: *How do you act under stress?*

⚬

An eye-opening statement by Rabbi Abraham ibn Ezra, in his commentary to the Torah, brings the message home.

The Torah states (*Bamidbar* 15:37-39):

> *And G-d spoke to Moses, saying, "Speak to the Children of Israel and say to them that they shall make for themselves fringes, [to be placed upon] the corners of their garments, for all their generations ...*

*and you will see it, and you will remember all the
commandments of G-d, and you will observe them."*

This refers to the *mitzvah* of *tzitzit*. We place fringes on the
four corners of a garment, as a sign. We see the fringes, and
we remember the *mitzvot*.

In his commentary on *Devarim* 22:12, Ibn Ezra states:

*According to my judgment, an individual is more obli-
gated to wear tzitzit at other times than during
prayers. So he will remember, and not err, and not sin
at any time. Since,* during prayers, a person will not sin.

We're concerned about your conduct in the real world – your
interactions with people, your performance under stress – *when
the going gets tough.* This is the litmus test of your character.

Let's face it. Nobody makes it through life without some
periods of adversity – whether they be financial, physical, or
emotional. Of course, nobody should ask for these difficulties,
and nobody enjoys them. But the right attitude during these
events makes a tangible difference. Your actions while you are
"under fire" show what you are made of.

As a start, remove the word "problem" from your vocabulary. Substitute the word "opportunity." Adversity presents us
with *opportunities*: to act properly under stress; to resist the
temptation to relax our standards; to pass a test.

∞

We'll close with a story. (Since this is based on memory, some details may not be exact.)

Rabbi Aharon Kotler, *zt"l*, was one of the giants of 20th-century Jewry. From his youth, his brilliant mind grasped material instantly. He grew to become respected throughout the world.

Once, a speaker provided a novel explanation of the following famous statement in *Pirkei Avot* (4:9):

> *Whoever, while in poverty, serves G-d, will someday serve Him in wealth.*

The speaker explained that the *poverty* and *wealth* referred to in the statement are not limited to finance. They can be explained in other terms as well: *intellectual* poverty, and *intellectual* wealth.

So whoever, despite being *intellectually poor* (unable to grasp quickly), studies Torah, will someday become *intellectually wealthy* – and, through his studies, develop his mental ability.

Rabbi Kotler, upon hearing this, cried. His reason: Since he was gifted intellectually even in his youth, *he never had such a test*.

He never had such a test!

In his mind, this was not "a problem avoided." This was "an opportunity missed."

So look at difficulty as an opportunity: to grow, to progress, to advance, and — *to pass the litmus test of good character.*

The Benefits of Gossip

WATCHING YOUR WORDS

Regarding a leper, the Torah (*Vayikra* 13:46) states: *All the days that the plague is upon him he will be considered impure. Indeed, he is impure. He must remain alone – outside the camp where he dwells.*

The Talmud (*Arachin* 16a)* comments:

> *Why is the leper different [from others who are impure] and he therefore must remain outside the camp of his residence? He separated [with the gossip he uttered] man and wife and man and his friend. Therefore, the Torah said that he must be separate.*

[A note of caution: The following is not to be taken at face value. It is intended, through the use of irony, to dramatize our message.]

*Attribution of the statement in the *Gemara* is as follows: *Rabbi Shmuel asked in the name of Rabbi Chanina. Some say it was Rabbi Shmuel bar Nadav, the son-in-law of Rabbi Chanina who asked of Rabbi Chanina; and some say he asked it of Rabbi Yehoshua ben Levi.*

We are all thoroughly familiar with the phrase "equal time." When one political candidate is provided with time to air his view, his opponent must be given an equal amount of time to express the opposing opinion.

Gossip (*lashon hara*) deserves equal time. After all, much has been said and written about the negative side of gossip. Clearly, gossip has its detractors. Should we not present the opposing view? Doesn't our sense of fairness mandate that we provide equal time to defend this practice? It must have *some* benefits:

(1) *Gossip is time efficient.*

One speaks *lashon hara* when one comments negatively about another individual – even if the comment is true.

The *Chafetz Chaim*, as the author of the definitive work on the subject is known, points out that one statement of *lashon hara* may involve numerous transgressions. Depending on the circumstance, a few choice words of *lashon hara* may transgress "Love your neighbor as you love yourself," or "Do not hate your brother in your heart," or "Do not place a stumbling block before a blind person" (that is, do not cause others – the listeners, in this case – to sin).

Let's not underestimate this. After all, we live in a fast-paced world. We eat fast food, we instantly fax our correspondence, we access computer-generated data at the touch of a button. Time is at a premium.

How convenient, then, is gossip! With one statement, we

can transgress a substantial number of prohibitions – accomplishing in a few short words, and in just a few seconds, what might have otherwise taken many a great deal of time to accomplish.

(2) *The victim need not be present.*

When an individual physically harms somebody, the results are before him. He faces his victim, and is fully aware of the damage that has been done. Conceivably, this sight could trigger regret. The sight of an individual in pain could arouse feelings of sympathy toward the person who has been injured.

Lashon hara does not have this problem. The victim need not be present. In fact, this individual can be many miles away. This permits the speaker to act with a clear conscience. Since the target of the remarks is out of view, the speaker can ignore the damage, and pretend that nobody is hurt. His or her conscience can remain clear, despite the damage that was done.

(3) *It provides the speaker with influence.*

In the course of our lives, we express views on many subjects. Often, these views have minimal impact upon others. They vie for attention with the multitude of thoughts and ideas which clutter the mind of the listener.

Lashon hara, on the other hand, has impact. If you say that a person is ignorant, clumsy, dishonest, or miserly, for example, your words carry weight. They create prejudice. When you successfully convey your words of gossip, your listeners will often prejudge the individual in question. Of course, this is based on your negative portrayal of that individual.

Even after becoming better acquainted with the person, the listener may never be fully detached from the view you provided. That ignorance, clumsiness, dishonesty, or miserliness will always appear to be present – thanks to your words.

(4) *It helps us to feel good about ourselves.*

Low self-esteem? Put down a friend.

Note this experiment: Subjects were put through a humiliating experience. Cards, neatly stacked, were rigged to tumble when the participants pulled a chair out from under a desk. Humiliated, the self-esteem of the subjects tumbled as well. The result? The participants of the study responded with hostility to attitude questions about others. They raised their self-esteem by putting others down.

How neatly *lashon hara* fits into the picture. It is clearly the most convenient method of denigrating others. It is, therefore, the put-down of choice among individuals with low self-worth.

What else can we say? If you are seeking a pursuit which is (1) time efficient; which (2) does not require the victim to be present; which (3) provides you with influence; and (4) helps you feel good about yourself at the expense of others – then, without question, *lashon hara* is for you!

Two Ships

DEALING WITH DEATH

How does one deal with death? How does one accept a personal loss? How does one come to terms with the grief and pain which result from losing somebody dear?

We can draw inspiration from the following parable:

There are two ships in the harbor. One is setting sail. The other is arriving in port after a long voyage. Great fanfare and excitement surround the departing ship, while the arriving ship is virtually unnoticed.

Yet which ship really deserves the celebration? *The arriving one*. After all, it has just completed a successful voyage. This is an accomplishment of considerable note. The departing ship, on the other hand, has yet to accomplish anything. Its future is unknown. Why should there be a celebration?

∞∞

The two ships represent two dimensions of a person's existence: birth and death.

Upon the birth of a child, there is a celebration. Yet that celebration is not based upon accomplishment – *it is based upon potential*. We hope and pray that the child will have a successful life.

Upon a person's death, however, *potential* is no longer important. Rather, it is a time to reflect upon what has *actually taken place*. When a person lives a meaningful life, his or her death becomes a time to reflect: How much has this person accomplished! It is a time to salute a voyage of success.

After a loss, one must pause to reflect upon the deceased's impact upon others. The mourners must listen with pride to the stories and incidents conveyed by visitors. Yes, the loss is difficult and overwhelming. However, the mourner can take solace in the thought that his or her loved one made an impact upon the world. Often, in fact, mourners find it difficult to believe that their dear relative could have done *so much* without people close to him or her being aware of it!

Among the most moving tragedies in the Torah is the sudden death of Nadav and Avihu, Aaron's two sons. When that occurred, the *Midrash* (*Vayikra Rabbah* 12:2) teaches us, Moses said to his brother, Aaron:

> *"My brother. I was told at Sinai that I would sanctify this home [the Tabernacle] and that it [the sanctification] would be through somebody important. I thought that it might be myself, or it might be you …*

now, I see that the two of them [Nadav and Avihu] are bigger than myself and bigger than you."

Once Aaron heard that his sons were [considered] G–d fearing, he was silent.

Knowing that the deceased lived for a purpose is highly meaningful to the mourner.

෴

What else must the mourner know? *That death does not really end life.*

At death, there is a marked contrast between the two entities which comprise the human being: the body and the soul. The body, the physical human being, is buried in the earth. Despite its years of life, it has no more to "show for itself" at death than it did at birth. As the Creator said to Adam (*Bereishit* 3:19):

"For you are dust, and to dust you will return."

Is not *everything* physical, *everything* material – just that way? In the end, is there anything lasting, anything enduring, from things which are physical or material?

On the other hand, there is the spiritual entity of life – the *neshamah*, the soul. Upon the death of a person, the *neshamah* remains. It is with G-d. *It is eternal.*

As is written in *Kohelet* (12:5,7):

For man is going back to his world ... and the dust will return to the land, as it was, and the spirit will go back to G-d.

In effect, only the physical life is over. The spiritual dimension of the person – the soul – lives on. Life has not ended. It has just taken a detour.

⚯

What else must the mourner know? *That he or she is not powerless to help the deceased.*

This is a concept that must be understood.

The *Zohar* states:

If the son [this, of course, would apply to the daughter as well] walks in the straight path and acts properly, he is definitely honoring his father [or mother] ... and the Holy One, Blessed Is He, has mercy upon [the deceased].

In other words, the deeds of the living elevate the deceased. The bond remains. There is still a link between the living and the dead. There is an invisible connection. This connection does not stop at the *Kaddish* that is recited by men. Rather, it extends to the realm of other *mitzvot*, which both men and women can perform to elevate the soul of the deceased.

⚯

In addition to all of the above, there is something else that a mourner should keep in mind: *That he or she is not alone.*

Years ago, in Aleppo, Syria, the Jewish community had a special carriage which carried the deceased to burial. On it was a quote from the Torah (*Shemot* 23:20):

> *Behold, I am sending an angel before you to guard you upon the road.*

Not only is the deceased guarded – the survivors are as well. Note this *mitzvah* from the Torah, regarding excessive mourning (*Devarim* 14:1):

> *You are the children of G-d. Do not cut yourselves, nor make baldness between your eyes, due to a death.*

On this, *Sforno* states in his commentary:

> *There is no reason to mourn excessively. G-d is your father, and you are His child. He will take care of you.*

It is important for the mourner to know that he or she is not alone, that there is a Creator, that there is a plan. The mourner must know that he or she will be taken care of. G-d is your Father, and you are His child.

May G-d console all of our mourners. May each mourner reflect upon his or her loved one – a proud ship, returning to port after a successful journey.

Of Mice and Men

ACKNOWLEDGING
THE DIVINE PLAN

Perhaps nothing represents the modern age more than the computer. This makes it even more difficult, then, to explain Y2K, the crisis of the year 2000.

Apparently, everybody overlooked something. It seems that computer software is designed to read only the last two digits of the number which designates a year. Consequently, 1997 is 97, 1998 is 98, and 1999 is 99.

So far, no problem.

However, the year 2000 is 00, and the year 2001 is 01. As a result, when the computer sequences these years, the order will be 00, 01, 97, 98, and 99. The years 2000 and 2001 will be ahead of the years 1997, 1998, and 1999.

This is a problem.

Nobody thought of this? Where were people of vision when these systems were designed? How could this possibly have been overlooked?

☙❧

We all know the story of The Tower of Bavel (*Bereishit*, Ch. 11). As most people understand it, a group of evil people wanted to build a tower to reach the heavens.

> *And they said, "Let us build a city and a tower — which will reach the heavens … lest we be dispersed throughout the world."*

The Creator did not like this. He said:

> *"Let us descend and confuse their language so that each person will not understand the language of his friend."*

Not all commentaries, however, agree on the nature of events. Ibn Ezra, in his commentary, and Rabbi David Kimchi, in his, do not view the intentions of the tower- builders as evil. These people simply wanted to build a tall tower that would be visible from afar – to glorify their city and give it a "name."

Why did the Creator frustrate their plans if those plans were not evil? Because it was not His intention that mankind should be concentrated in one location on the earth. Rather, it was His intention that mankind "be fruitful and multiply" and fill the earth. So the plan of the tower-builders was not to be.

All the best-laid plans *of mice and men …*

This brings to mind a statement in *Mishlei* (19:21):

Many are the intentions of man. However, the Will of God – that is what lasts.

Now, back to the computer. It is as if G-d said, again, *"Let us go down and confuse their language."* This time it is the language of the computer. It is as if He is telling us that, regardless of all our technology, there is still a G-d Who controls the world. There is a Divine Plan.

In the same vein is something that happened in a recent year at the Comdex computer trade show. Bill Gates was demonstrating his new Windows 98 software. Now, let us remember that Bill Gates is by far the biggest name in the computer industry, and his new software is much anticipated, and is no doubt state of the art.

What happened during the demonstration? *The system crashed.*

The best-laid plans of mice and men …

There is a fundamental difference between the man or the woman of *emunah* (faith) and the person who has no faith at all. Faith causes an individual to view the world in a certain unique light. Belief in a Creator is accompanied by an understanding that events happen for a reason – that there is a Divine plan. That plan can allow something, whose chances are slim, to succeed. Conversely, it can cause something, that is almost guaranteed of success, to fail.

All we need do is observe the world scene. There is no shortage of examples.

Take modern medicine, for example. Amidst all the advances, all the cures and all the preventions of modern technology, *a new disease has been added*. It is known as AIDS.

Take meteorology. Despite all the advances, *we still cannot control the weather.*

In all fields, examples abound. Despite the march of technology, despite the plans of brilliant men, *"the Will of G-d – that is what lasts."* This, despite the plans *of mice and men.*

Crash!

PATIENCE

Following an airplane crash, much effort is made to determine the cause. Central to that effort, usually, are the "black boxes" that had been aboard the flight. These units contain valuable flight data and often help to uncover the cause of the crash.

Recently, an intriguing proposal was announced: to install "black boxes" in automobiles.

We can readily understand their value. Following an accident, authorities would analyze the data. As is the case with airplanes, the information could be critical in determining the cause of the crash.

Now, a thought: Airplanes can crash. Automobiles can crash. And *people* can crash, as well – spiritually, that is.

We see it all the time. The individual "takes off" toward greater spiritual heights. There is great potential, great promise. Then, C-R-A-S-H!!! Suddenly it's over.

If we could analyze an imaginary "black box" – filled with thought data from these individuals – what lessons would we learn? Why, indeed, do people crash?

When the Children of Israel were enslaved in Egypt, Moses was directed by G-d (*Shemot* 3:10):

> *"Now go, and I will send you to Pharaoh, and take My nation, the Children of Israel, out of Egypt."*

Following this, the Children of Israel had high hopes (*Shemot* 4:31):

> *And the nation believed. They heard that G-d remembered the Children of Israel ... and they bowed.*

Then Moses approached Pharaoh, carrying the word of G-d. Did this result in freedom? Or, at least, did it alleviate the burden which the Egyptians had placed upon the Jewish people? Not exactly (*Shemot* 5:6,7):

> *And Pharaoh commanded ..., "No longer should you give straw to the nation to make bricks, as previously. Now let them go and gather straw for themselves."*

Not only was their burden not alleviated, but it became greater.

The people were stunned. This was not what they expected. Their response to Moses was angry (*Shemot* 5:21):

> *"You have placed a sword in the hands of Pharaoh, to kill us."*

This was quite a change from "And the nation believed"! What had happened? The people had expected immediate results. They had not expected to sacrifice. So they went from a spiritual high to a spiritual low.

In effect, *they crashed.*

In people's lives today, this is even more pronounced. After all, as is well known, we live in an age of instant gratification. People expect immediate benefit, instant pleasure. They expect this from material things. And, it seems, they expect this spiritually, as well.

Some scenarios:

- **The *chesed* crash.** A young woman attends a day of inspiration on the subject of *chesed* – acts of kindness. She is moved by what she hears. She is determined to make *chesed* a part of her life. Overflowing with enthusiasm, she becomes a volunteer. She will work with people, and improve their lives.

  Three months later, this "volunteer" is nowhere to be found. Yes, she did begin her project. Yes, she did make some effort. But the enthusiasm cooled. The determination faded.

  C-R-A-S-H!!!

  Why? Because she was unprepared for sacrifice. Because she expected instant results. The emotional gratification, the sense of success, was not immediate. The lives of the people she worked with did not turn around so quickly.

Things were taking too long.

- **The *tefillah* crash.** He hears about "the power of prayer" and he resolves to use it. After all, his life has not been proceeding according to plan. Things are not the way he would like them to be. *Tefillah* (prayer) seems like a good idea.

  Six months later – you guessed it – *nothing*. Why? Well, the first week he prayed, nothing changed. He was stunned. The second week, there was some change – but it was not enough. This was not what he had expected. C-R-A-S-H!!!

- **The *learning* crash.** He resolves to add Torah to his life. He is *kovei'a ittim*, studying regularly. He rises early, every day, and attends a *shiur,* a class, in Talmud.

  At first he feels enormously uplifted. He is glowing. But after a while the glow dims. He has difficulty absorbing all the material, and he has difficulty remembering what he does absorb.

  True, with work, he could achieve results. True, with some review, he could absorb all the material and even remember it. But, he wonders, should it be this difficult? Should it require such work?

  He was not prepared for the sacrifice. C-R-A-S-H!!!

∽∾

As teachers, as parents, the fault may be ours. Anxious to encourage others to do *mitzvot*, we make promises, even guarantees. And, while doing so, we fail to warn of the sacrifices involved. Whether it be *chesed,* or prayer, or study, results may take time.

Of course, during the wait there is still the satisfaction, even the glow, of the *mitzvah* itself. *The reward of a mitzvah is the mitzvah!* We are, after all, carrying out the Will of the Creator, and we are injecting *kedushah*, holiness, into our lives. This is not insignificant.

Regarding other results, keep in mind the following: Results, often, eventually come. As was the case with the Jews in Egypt in the incident mentioned above, the final result was indeed successful – but it took time.

Regarding prayer, for example, it is written in *Tehillim* (27:14):

Pray to G-d. Strengthen your heart. And pray to G-d.

Our Sages tell us: If your prayer is not answered, pray again. Results may not be immediate. The same could be the case with *chesed*, with study, or with any potential change in our lives.

Be prepared to sacrifice. If results are not immediate, be patient. Remember: Planes may crash. Automobiles may crash. And *people may crash*, as well.

Books Without Pages

LEARNING FROM OTHERS

A number of years ago, a law was passed in New York mandating that operators of motorcycles wear helmets. Soon after the law was passed, a motorcycle operator was stopped by a police officer. He was told that he would be given a ticket.

"Why?" asked the driver.

"Because you are operating a motorcycle without a helmet," said the officer.

"That is not so," said the driver. He pointed to a helmet that was strapped onto his knee.

The police officer did not appreciate the man's sense of humor, and he wrote the ticket.

The time came for the driver's day in court. "You are charged with operating a motorcycle without a helmet. How do you plead?"

"Not guilty, Your Honor."

"Does that mean that you *were* wearing a helmet?"

"Yes, Your Honor, I was. It was on my knee."

The judge decided to be lenient. "I will let you go," he said. "But you must promise me that in the future you will wear the helmet *on your head.*" The man agreed.

The man left the courthouse, placed the helmet upon his head, hopped onto his motorcycle, and drove off.

Later, the man was in an accident *and injured his knee.*

In life, each of us channels our energies into pursuits which we consider to be important. In doing so, however, we often neglect other pursuits which are equally so.

Torah Study is the foundation of Jewish life. Yet few people realize that there are two types of study: one into which we invest much effort, and one into which, unfortunately, most of us do not.

When you think of "Torah Study," what picture comes into your mind? Undoubtedly, you visualize a person – a man, a woman, or a child – with an open book. That book may be a huge *Gemara* (volume of Talmud), a *Chumash* (one of the Five Books of the Torah), or perhaps a book of laws. But, likely, there is a book in the picture that is in your mind.

Indeed, much of what we learn is from books. Such study is our love and our treasure. It is one of the hallmarks of the Jewish people. But there is a second type of Torah study.

During the journey of the Jewish people through the desert, they passed through a place called Marah. Regarding this place, the Torah (*Shemot* 15:25) states:

> *There, He [G-d] gave them chok [law] and mishpat [justice].*

To what does this refer? Ramban (Nachmanides) explains: *Chok* and *mishpat* do not refer to specific laws and judgments. Rather, they refer to general rules of conduct. The people were taught how to conduct themselves. They were taught how to withstand adversity, how to properly make requests from the Creator (instead of complaining). They were taught, as well, how to love others, how to take advice from elders, how to be humble, and how to act toward visitors to the camp.

Why was this necessary? After all, concepts like these are included in the Torah, which the Jewish people were soon to receive. Why could they not learn them from there?

Because you cannot learn everything from a book. Delicate nuances of behavior cannot easily be conveyed through the written word. Proper conduct can often only be learned through personal contact, from people with knowledge – from *books without pages.*

Few people recognize this. As a result, they ignore the priceless knowledge that can only be gained from personal contact with the right people.

Who are the people from whom we should learn?
First, Torah scholars.

The *Gemara* (*Berachot* 47b) has an interesting discussion. The subject: Who is an *am ha'aretz* (unlearned person)?

A number of answers are given:

(1) One who does not read Shema twice daily.

(2) One who does not wear tefillin.

(3) One who does not have tzitzit on his garment.

(4) One who does not have a mezuzah upon his door.

(5) Whoever has sons and does not teach them Torah.

Thus far all opinions are quite basic. Now, let us look at opinion number six:

(6) Even one who learned and reviewed his learning – but did not serve [or, spend time with] Torah scholars – is an unlearned person.

He is an *am ha'aretz* even if he learned and reviewed – because you cannot learn everything from books.

Interestingly, Rashi notes that learning *Gemara* serves the purpose of being with Torah scholars (because it helps us to understand that which was already written). After quoting Rashi, Rabbi Moshe Feinstein (*Igrot Moshe, Y. D.* 4:32) notes:

Even though, in our day, the Gemara and other works which were formerly oral are now in writing, there is still a Torah that is unwritten, and it is not possible to know this Torah well without serving Torah scholars.

Torah scholars – rabbis and other *talmidei chachamim* – are *books without pages*. They are filled with knowledge.

Contact with them provides us with knowledge that cannot be acquired anyplace else.

∞∞

We can also learn from the elderly.

The Torah commands us to respect the elderly. Regarding this, the Sages (*Kiddushin* 33a) state:

> *This refers to all elderly people [not just learned ones]... Rabbi Yochanan would stand when an elderly Aramean passed by. He [Rabbi Yochanan] explained: ìHow many trials and tribulations they [people such as this one] have had in their lives!"*

The *Gemara* continues to explain that the sage Rabbah would not actually stand, but would do some action to show respect. In any case, the statement of Rabbi Yochanan stands: "How many trials and tribulations have they had in their lives!"

Why do their trials and tribulations make them deserving of respect? The *Chatam Sofer* explains: *"From their life experiences, they acquire wisdom."*

If this is the case with somebody who does not have much spiritual knowledge, how much more is it the case with somebody who does! Elders – whose years have been steeped in Jewish tradition, who have looked at their life experiences with the wise eyes of a man or woman of faith – are ever-flowing fountains of knowledge. How could we fail to take advantage of them?

〜

Another source of knowledge is our friends.
In *Pirkei Avot* (4:1) we learn:

> *Ben Zoma stated: "Who is wise? One who learns from every man."*

Our Sages emphasize that this refers to people who know less than we do, as well as people who know more. If a person has the humility to learn even from those who have less knowledge than he or she does, then the sincerity of such learning is obvious. What a huge, untapped source of knowledge this is! Stop for a few moments, consider each of your friends and relatives, and find at least one good trait that you can learn from each of them.

Let us rethink things. Let us realize that in addition to the all-important, nuts-and-bolts study of the printed word, there are other sources of wisdom that must be tapped. People – sages, elders, even ordinary friends and acquaintances – can be the source of much knowledge and growth. Let us take full advantage of this. Let us learn from books with pages, and let us learn from books without them. Unlike our friend on the motorcycle, let us not concentrate on one at the expense of the other.

Give-and-Take

GIVING WITH SENSITIVITY

Giving is admirable. Often, however, *as we give, we also take away*.

First, let us discuss *giving*.

A few years ago, at a Thanksgiving Day Parade in Manhattan, something like the following took place:

An observer, viewing the parade from an upper-floor vantage point in a building along the route, leaned over a bit too far and fell through an open window.

On the ground below, among the thousands of spectators, stood a man who was observing the parade together with his young son – *balloon in hand*. The upper-floor observer landed upon this man. Fortunately, neither was seriously hurt. And the parade continued as planned.

Later, somebody asked the father, regarding his son, "What did *he* think of all this?"

The man replied, "He was upset that his balloon had burst."

❧

The young child's behavior serves as a metaphor to that of many adults. As events swirl around them, as the lives of others are battered by difficulties, some people show no sensitivity, no concern. Self-centered, they are involved – obsessed, even – only with their own lives, their personal interests. They are distressed only when *their own* balloon has burst.

The Torah, of course, stands the self-centered attitude upon its head. It instructs us to be sensitive, to consider the needs of others – even during times of personal stress. It instructs us to constantly be looking after the needs of others.

As the Sage Rabbi Simlai (*Sotah* 14a) stated:

> *The Torah begins with chesed [kindness] and ends with chesed ... [The Torah begins with G-d creating garments for Adam and Eve, and ends with the burial of Moses.]*

We focus upon what we can give, not upon what we can take. We must, however, go even beyond this, and realize the following: Sometimes, even as we give, we take something away.

Consider, for example, somebody whose financial status has declined. Until now, let us say, he has earned a handsome living, was self-sufficient, and even generously gave to worthy causes. Now he has no income, and is seriously in need of assistance. You decide, admirably, to help. You resolve to provide this individual with the assistance he requires. *You are prepared to give*.

If, however, you are not careful, even as you *give*, you will be *taking away* – his pride, his self-esteem, and his sense of worth. If you *are* careful, on the other hand, your noble act can be all *giving*. Nothing will detract from it. There will be no *taking away*.

⊂⊙⊃

Let us step back for a moment to reflect upon this message.

In the minds of some people, the very fact that an act of *chesed* is performed – in any way, shape or form – is an accomplishment worthy of note. When they perform such an act, they feel, they are way ahead of many others, who do little or nothing to help people in need.

This is true. But it is not enough. After inspiring ourselves to perform the *chesed* in the first place, we must then take pains to plan it properly, with care and precision, fine-tuning every move in consideration of the delicate emotions of the person on the receiving end.

The following are some role models (as noted in *Midrash Ruth Rabbah*):

(1) *Boaz*: According to Torah Law, bundles of grain, which are left behind in harvesting, are designated for the poor.

As noted in *Megillat Ruth* (2:16), when Boaz, the landowner, saw Ruth, impoverished and seeking nourishment, he directed his men thus:

> *"And also intentionally let bundles fall, and leave them there, and she will gather."*

Boaz could have personally approached Ruth and given her as much grain as she required. However, giving her grain in that manner would be taking away her dignity. Boaz therefore chose to exercise care and sensitivity, and found a way to give – *without taking away.*

(2) *Rabbi Yochanan:* He intentionally dropped coins, so Rabbi Shimon bar Ba (who was poor) would find them.

(3) *Rabbi Yehudah HaNasi*: He intentionally "lost" kernels of grain, so Rabbi Shimon ben Chalafta would find them.

In all these cases, a way was found to give, without taking away. Help was given, though no dignity was removed.

We can apply these principles to everyday scenarios:

- A person requires financial help. You build his confidence with the words, "I know you'll repay me soon."

- A friend asks for a favor. You state, "I'm honored that you feel close enough to ask."
- You do something for an acquaintance. You say, "It's the least I could do for all you've done for me."

One point to consider is this: You're going to do the *chesed*, in any case. Why not maximize its effect by doing it with the proper disposition?

Remember: Many a person is concerned only with self. Many an individual is obsessed with personal gain. We must do better. We must perform acts of *chesed*, and perform them with care and sensitivity. Our actions should be all *giving* and no *taking away*.

Consider the needs and emotions of others. Get involved — even if the balloon that has burst is not your own.

Okay!!!

ENTHUSIASM IN PERFORMING *MITZVOT*

The word *okay* carries a variety of connotations. They range from lukewarm to enthusiastic:*

> *Lukewarm:* "How was the book?" "Nothing special. It was just *okay*."
> *Positive:* "How do you feel?" "I feel fine. I'm *okay*."
> *Enthusiastic:* "How did your team do yesterday?" "Okay!!!" (They won easily.)

Same word, different meanings.

We can draw upon these shades of meaning to frame a message about *mitzvot*.

Commonly, when an individual seeks to evaluate his or her commitment to Torah and *mitzvot*, the following questions

---

*As pointed out in *The Mother Tongue*, by Bill Bryson.

are asked: *How many mitzvot do I observe? Am I performing as many mitzvot as I should?*

Commitment, however, carries an additional component, one that is often overlooked.

That component is *intensity.* It is not sufficient to ask about the *quantity* of *mitzvot* we are performing. Each of us must also ask, "What is the *intensity* of my observance? What enthusiasm do I bring to the performance of *mitzvot?* How much feeling, how much fervor, how much passion, how much love do I feel and display in carrying out the commandments of the Torah? Is my level of intensity just 'okay,' or is it filled with enthusiasm and passion, making it: 'OKAY!!!'?"

Let us focus upon a statement – a startling one – by the Talmudic Sage, Rav.

In *Yirmiyahu* 9:12, it is stated:

> *Why was the land [of Israel] lost? G-d said, "Because they [the Jewish people] have forsaken My Torah."*

The statement appears to be self-explanatory. But Rav, as quoted by Rabbi Yehudah (*Nedarim* 81a), notes:

> *They did not say a berachah [blessing] before studying.*

How is this to be understood? Is this reason enough for the land to be lost? Is this reason enough to exile the Jewish people from their homeland?

Rashi explains:

> *In their failure to recite the blessings, they showed that the Torah, to them, is not an important gift.*

Understood. But we still wonder. After all, they were nevertheless engaged in studying Torah. Should they be exiled?

Our answer: as long as they were studying, *no*. But their lack of love, their lack of intensity, signaled the beginning of the end.

We can illustrate this with a comparison.

In the laws of *netilat yadayim* (ritual washing of hands), it is often important to know if the hands of a person are considered to be dry or wet. How much moisture must be upon a person's hands for them to be *halachically* wet? The *halachic* standard is known as *tofeyach al menat lehatfiyach*, which means, *wet enough to wet something else*. In other words, if the hands are moist, but not moist enough to wet something else, they are not *halachically* wet. It is as if they are dry.

Study of Torah conforms to this model. When there is love, when there is intensity, the feeling radiates and captures the imagination of others. But when the study of Torah is mechanical, when it is dry, there is no *tofeyach al menat lehatfiyach*; there is not enough to transfer to others. Intensity, enthusiasm, and love are contagious.

We now understand what Rashi may have been alluding to. The failure to say a blessing upon the study of Torah reflected a lack of love. That lack of love left nothing to be transferred to others. This was the beginning of the end.

This is the case with all the *mitzvot*. If we perform them in a dry, mechanical fashion, there is limited effect upon those around us. If, on the other hand, we perform our *mitzvot* with feeling, then others are moved. Our love, our passion for *mitzvot,* inspires others. Intensity radiates. Enthusiasm is contagious.

Let us each, therefore, ask ourselves these questions:

- Are my prayers recited with feeling?
- Is my *Shabbat* table a true hub of animated spiritual give-and-take?
- Is my study of Torah a labor of love?
- Are my acts of *chesed* (kindness) thought of as a privilege, not a burden – when I give to the needy? When I visit the sick?
- Do I work on the performance of each *mitzvah* – to carry it out with love, intensity, and feeling?

From here on in, let us not simply ask, "How many *mitzvot* do I perform?" Let us also ask, "What level of intensity do I have?"

Let our observance be more than "okay." Let it be filled with passion, with love, with feeling. Let it be *"OKAY!!!"*

Streaks

ACHIEVING CONSISTENCY

Don't be overly impressed.

On September 6, 1995, Cal Ripken, Jr., of the Baltimore Orioles, made baseball history: *He played in his 2,131st consecutive ball game.* In doing so, he eclipsed the streak of the legendary Lou Gehrig, the Iron Man of Baseball.

Ripken's streak spanned fourteen seasons. During that time, he played in every game. Neither injury nor illness nor any other distraction deterred him from fulfilling his responsibility to his team.

The world took notice. In an era that thirsts for dedication and consistency, Ripken's streak is an outstanding example of both.

We feel, however, that you should not be overly impressed. As Jews who are committed to Torah and *mitzvot, we live with streaks at all times.* Performing an action – an admirable one, a *mitzvah* – in consecutive fashion, without missing once, is something we accept gladly as our obligation. It is not something that we feel deserves special mention.

Dedication? It is all around us. Consistency? It, too, abounds among our people. Iron Men, Iron Women? We have plenty.

How do we explain this?

∽◌∽

One of our classic commentators provides us with an important insight:

In *Parashat Ki Teitzei* (*Devarim* 22:1), the Torah instructs us regarding the return of a lost object:

> *Do not see the ox of your friend or his sheep, which have lost their way – and look aside. Rather, return them, return them, to your brother.*

The Torah wanted to merit the Jewish people with the *mitzvah* of *ve'ahavta lerei'acha kamocha* (loving your fellow man as you love yourself) and to make it take root within them. It therefore obligated us to perform this *mitzvah*.

Taking root, however, does not happen instantly. Consequently, the Torah repeats its instructions:

> *Return them, return them, to your brother.*

The *Alshich* states:

> *The first time, you will return it to fulfill the commandment of the Torah. The next time, you will do so on your own.*

If you have performed a *mitzvah* once, you will naturally do so a second time. It works this way: When a person performs a *mitzvah* which he or she had never done before, a barrier is torn down. Once this is accomplished, the stage is set for the *mitzvah* to be carried out again and again, each time with less resistance. After performing the *mitzvah* once, you will naturally do so a second time.

In the words of the Sage Ben Azzai (*Avot* 4:2):

A mitzvah brings another mitzvah.

With the commandment of the Torah providing the obligation, and repetition of the deed whittling away at our internal resistance, performing a *mitzvah* – consistently, consecutively, without missing even once – is within our reach.

Streaks, therefore, abound.

Among our people there are:

- the elderly grandfather who has attended *minyan* on thousands of consecutive mornings – may he do so until 120;
- the man of middle age, now gray at the temples, who has uttered blessings upon the last 20,000 foods he ate;
- the young mother who has lit candles on 150 consecutive Fridays – and expects to do so for thousands more;
- the Jewish teenager who resisted hundreds of opportunities, of all types, to do the wrong thing;
- the second-grader who shared his last 20 candy bars with a friend;

- the lawyer who checked 30 consecutive three-piece suits for *shaatnez;*
- the businessman who resisted hundreds of opportunities to deceive a customer;
- the mourner who never missed a *Kaddish*;
- all the people who never missed a chance to help the poor, invite a guest, console the bereaved, lend a hand, provide encouragement, give advice, or just be there for somebody.

It is important that we note the following: The most important threshold in a streak is its beginning. When you perform a *mitzvah* for the first time, you tear down a barrier, and pave the way for performance of the *mitzvah* again and again. Never take the performance of a *mitzvah* lightly: It could actually be the forerunner of many repeat performances.

So let us salute Mr. Ripken's accomplishment. But let us not be overly impressed. We are a People of Iron Men. We are a People of Iron Women.

Streaks, to us, are nothing new.

Lions

FAITH DURING CRISES

Ben was down and out. It was months since he had last received a paycheck. His savings were dwindling, and he was hard pressed to feed his family. He needed work.

One day a sign caught his eye: "MAN WANTED." He stepped back and realized that he was outside a circus. "Man wanted"? He decided to inquire.

Ben stepped inside and asked about the position.

"It's quite simple," he was told. "We dress you in the skin of a lion. You pretend that you are indeed the King of the Jungle, and you enter a cage with a live lion."

Ben turned to leave.

"You don't understand," he was told. "The lion is perfectly tame."

Against his better judgment, Ben accepted the job. After all, a good Jewish man must sacrifice for his family. And besides, "the lion is perfectly tame."

It was time for the main event. Ben put on the costume and stepped inside the cage. He circled about, as a lion would, and in fact grew quite comfortable in his role — until the cage sprang open. Before him was a four-legged creature that appeared to be anything but tame. The lion roared, scratched the floor with its paws, and roared again.

Then the lion turned toward Ben. It pawed the floor of the cage once again, and crouched back, ready to leap.

Ben decided that the end was near. If his life was indeed about to expire, he had better end it as a good Jew – with *Shema* on his lips.

He cried out, *"Shema Yisrael Hashem Elokeinu Hashem Echad."*

To which the other lion replied, *"Baruch Shem Kevod Malchuto Le'olam Va'ed."*

The "lion" of our tale represents a crisis in a person's life. Crises can be intimidating, regardless of their nature. Whether the crisis originates from illness or physical injury, from financial difficulty, from personal handicap, from difficulty in getting married or staying married, or whether it is a crisis in raising a child – it can be quite threatening.

Sometimes, in fact, there appears to be little hope.

The person of faith, however, must view events in a different light. To the man, the woman, of faith – to the individual with true *emunah* – nothing is intimidating. Yes, there is a crisis. Yes, it must be confronted. But what appears to be fierce may be nothing of the kind. What appears to be a "lion" may be something much more tame.

⬥

When the Jewish people were enslaved in Egypt, Pharaoh issued a decree against newborn male children (*Shemot* 1:22):

"Any son who is born must be thrown into the Nile."

While the decree was in effect, Moses was born and was hidden for three months. Then (*Shemot* 2:3-4):

And she [his mother] could not hide him any longer, and she took a basket ... and placed the child into it, and placed it into the reeds at the edge of the Nile. And his sister stood in the distance, to see what would happen to him.

The *Maharsha* (*Sotah* 11a) explains this symbolically. The "sister" represents the *Shechinah* (the Presence of the Creator). And "standing in the distance" represents His wisdom, hidden and distant from the understanding of mankind.

The Creator was there. *The child was not alone.*

Nor are *we* alone in our crises. Though they may be beyond our understanding, though they may appear to be unsolvable, – we must realize that there is much that we do not see. There is a Divine Plan. The Creator stands in the distance. Crises can be conquered.

The lion is not fierce at all.

The Seven Habits of Spiritually Ineffective People

WHY PEOPLE FAIL

In recent years, self-help books have gained substantially in popularity. Among the more successful of these volumes is *The Seven Habits of Highly Effective People,* by Steven R. Covey.

The allure of such a book is understandable. People who are seeking to advance themselves are intensely interested in the secrets of success of those who have already done so. Effective people have distinct habits which help them to succeed and excel.

By the same token, *ineffective people – spiritually* ineffective people – have their own unique habits. It is these habits which keep them from advancing. It is these habits which help them to fail.

We hereby present "The Seven Habits of Spiritually Ineffective People." These habits are based upon the incidents involving Adam and Eve in the Garden of Eden, and Cain's conflict with Abel.

(1) *They choose their friends carefully, associating only with people who do not advance.*

We naturally gauge our own actions by the actions of friends. When we see a friend growing as a Jew, we are often inspired to do the same.

People who want to elevate themselves make certain that they are surrounded by friends seeking to do the same. A person who, on the other hand, chooses to maintain a spiritual status quo is careful to associate only with people who do not grow. Why be inspired? Why subject oneself to the discomforting feeling that more could be done? Why open the door to becoming a better person?

Some friends go even further: They actively encourage a person to do the wrong thing.

In the incident involving Adam and Eve, the serpent influences the woman, and the woman influences the man. The rest is history.

(2) *They believe that their religion deprives them of something important.*

The observant Jew is committed to a life of *mitzvot*. He, she, as a person of faith, feels *privileged* to observe the Torah, and understands that both the positive commandments and the restrictions elevate, enhance, and sanctify our lives.

Not so the spiritually ineffective person. Far from it. He, she, constantly wonders: *What am I missing?* *What is the Torah depriving me of?* *How much do the restrictions of Judaism detract from my life?*

This point of view is clearly represented in the words of the serpent to Eve, in encouraging her to eat from the tree (*Bereishit* 3:5):

> *"… for G-d knows that on the day you eat from it [the tree], your eyes will be opened, and you will be like G-d, knowing good from evil."*

Or, in other words: "G-d is holding something back from you. You're missing out."

(3) *They are determined to ignore the long-term effects of their actions and lifestyle.*

People who succeed spiritually – individuals who work to constantly enhance the level of *kedushah* (holiness) in their lives – understand that even the simplest deeds have long-term impact. Consequently, they forgo momentary temptation, or withstand momentary difficulty, in order to do what is best for themselves and their family in the long run.

People who, on the other hand, are spiritually ineffective do the opposite. They magnify the needs of the moment, and ignore the needs of the future. They see only what is on the surface – as did Eve in eating from the tree (*Bereishit* 3:6):

> *And the woman saw that the tree would be good to eat from, that it was desirous to the eyes, and magnificent to behold.*

Her decision was a superficial one.

(4) *They creatively blame everybody but themselves for their failures.*

The person who seeks to advance understands that nobody is perfect, that everybody makes mistakes. To grow, you acknowledge your errors and take steps to avoid repeating them.

The spiritually ineffective person, on the other hand, is different. Interested in making the same mistakes over and over again? Then don't admit that you made them in the first place. Simply blame others, not yourself – as did Adam and Eve (*Bereishit* 3:12-13):

> *And the man said, "The woman whom you gave to be with me--she gave me from the tree, and I ate"... And the woman said, "The snake deceived me, and I ate."*

(5) *They tirelessly search for shortcuts to Heaven.*

Judaism requires twenty-four-hours-a-day self-discipline. There are no magic solutions that allow us to let down our guard. There are no special dispensations that allow us to bypass the rules.

The spiritually ineffective person refuses to accept this. He, she, is always seeking a magical solution that allows bypassing the hard work of being a Jew. A prayer, a ritual, an amulet – something, anything – as long as it does not require self-discipline or hard work. Where, oh where, is that shortcut to Heaven?

In the case of Cain and Abel: Abel's sacrifice is accepted, according to the commentary of Rav Ovadia Sforno, because *Abel* was pleasing, as was his offering. And the reverse would hold true for Cain: Both he and his offering were unacceptable.

The text does not say: *"And to Cain's offering G-d did not turn."* Rather, it says (*Bereishit* 4:5):

And to Cain and his offering G-d did not turn.

Cain and his offering were one. If the person is not what he should be, there is no magic offering that will make everything right.

(6) *They maintain their focus – they dwell on the past.*

The Torah continues (*Bereishit* 4:6):

And G-d said to Cain, "Why are you distressed?"

As Rav Sforno explains G-d's words to Cain: When something that is wrong can be fixed, *there is no reason to agonize over the past.* Rather, one should work toward improving in the future. The spiritually healthy person learns from the past to improve the future. The spiritually infirm person irrationally dwells on the past and agonizes over it, yet does not take encouragement from the future that is ahead and the promise that is held within it.

(7) *They staunchly refuse to listen to advice.*

To grow as a Jew is to be constantly open to advice. To remain static as a Jew is to close one's ears to words that make one grow.

G-d spoke to Cain, providing him with the thoughts he required to put his life in order. Cain's reaction? There is none. He is not open to advice.

∞∞

Look back, please, at the *seven habits*. Do any of them describe you? If so, is there something you could do to change?

Remember: Effective people have developed habits which help them to continue to advance and grow. And ineffective people – *spiritually ineffective people* – have their own unique habits which help them to avoid growth, withstand inspiration, and avoid the challenge of spiritually enhancing their lives.

How Important Is It?

KEEPING LIFE IN PERSPECTIVE

The traveler had only heard about it. Now, he would be able to experience it firsthand: the ice-sculpting contest in the desert.

He watched the sculptors as they worked. One was crafting a miniature city. Another was designing a medieval castle. Still another was sculpting a city skyline.

All the artists were diligent. All were quite careful. Each put hammer and chisel to the ice with painstaking detail.

The traveler, though impressed, was puzzled.

He said to one of the sculptors, "This is the desert. The temperature is 120 degrees Fahrenheit. All this effort, all this work, is useless. Everything is going to melt."

The artist replied, "Don't you think we know that? We are fully aware that none of the sculptures will last."

The sculptor continued, pointing, "Take a look at the sign that is hanging over there."

For the first time, the visitor noticed the sign. It read: HOW IMPORTANT IS IT?

The speaker explained, "That is our theme. In life, we go through a great deal of stress. Many things upset us. If something hurts us financially, we are upset. If something is a blow to our egos, it upsets us. If we are not given the respect we would like to have, we become upset. This ice-sculpting contest reminds us to ask, each time we are upset, "Does this really matter? Should I really be distressed? Years from now, will it mean anything?

How important is it?

In *Pirkei Avot* (6:9) it is written:

When somebody leaves this world, not his silver, nor his gold, nor his precious stones, nor his jewels, will accompany him. Rather, he is accompanied by his Torah and his good deeds.

We can underline this point with a variation on a well-known parable:

A man was faced with the prospect of pleading his case before the king. He resolved to ask each of his three groups of friends to accompany him. He asked the first group. They refused to accompany him. He asked the second group. They, too, refused to accompany him. Then he asked the third group. They replied, "Certainly we will accompany you. And we will remain with you to argue your case before the king."

The first group of friends represents our material possessions. We invest much effort in acquiring them. Yet, after "120 years," they are of no value to us.

The second group of friends represents our egos. Though we invest much in them during our lifetimes, they, too, do nothing for us after our stay here is over.

The third group of friends represents our Torah and *mitzvot*. Indeed, *they* are permanent, and "accompany " us even after our lives are over.

അൟ

In life, people become upset over all kinds of things which, in the long run, are not very important, and which, after it's all over, are not going to be so critical. Like an ice sculpture in the desert, they have no lasting value.

Take, for example, financial conflicts between people. Sometimes these differences are over relatively small sums. Yet they are the source of much stress.

How important is it?

Another source of stress is, believe it or not, happy occasions. People get upset over all kinds of details. The photographs were not exactly as they should have been; the video could have been better; the tablecloths did not match the dresses.

How important is it?

Recently, a major-league ballplayer misplayed three balls in one game. He was distressed. Later, he went home and watched *The Diary of Anne Frank*. This put things into focus for him. It made him put the game into perspective:

How important was it?

Another source of stress is ego and pride.

- Is it upsetting to you when you do not get the proper respect?
- Does it bother you when somebody gets credit for something – though *you* did most of the work?
- How irritating is it when somebody acts as if he or she is an expert on a certain subject – yet knows only 10 percent of what *you* know about it?

Before you get upset, ask yourself this question: *How important is it?*

To understand the next parable, the following should be noted: A man wears a *tallit* when he prays. It is also traditional that a man is buried in a *tallit*.

Now, the parable:

One day, as a man passed a certain house, he heard crying. He followed the sounds into the home. However, he saw nobody there. Soon he realized that the cries were originating from the upper floor. So he ascended the stairs, and followed the cries into the bedroom. But nobody was there. He listened closely, and followed the cries to a drawer in that room. He opened the drawer, and realized that the cries *were coming from a tallit!*

The man asked the *tallit*, "Why are you crying?"

The *tallit* answered, "My master went on vacation. He took his bathing trunks. He took his golf clubs. And he took his tennis racket. But me, his *tallit*, he left here."

The man answered the *tallit* as follows: "Don't worry. After '120 years,' your master will be going on another 'vacation.' Then, he will not be taking his bathing trunks. He will not be taking his golf clubs. And he will not be taking his tennis racket. But, you, his *tallit*, he indeed will be taking along."

Let's get our priorities straight. Let's realize what has value and what does not. Like ice sculptures in the desert, much of what we invest time and effort into – material things, pride, and ego – will someday "melt."

Before getting upset, ask yourself the question:

How important is it?

A Grandmother's Letter

WHERE HAS MODESTY GONE?

Dear Sarah,

I received your letter today with much happiness. You are a very special young lady. I am proud to be your grandmother.

You write: "I have experienced fifteen years of Torah education, from preschool through seminary. If there was any single theme that was emphasized the most, it was the theme of *tzniut* (modesty in dress)."

You continue: "Modesty, I was taught, is a hallmark of the observant Jewish woman."

You ask: "Where has it gone? How can our girls, our women, openly violate even the most minimal standards of feminine modesty? How, my dear grandmother, can we possibly explain the distressing decline in modest dress?"

My dear Sarah! You have touched upon a subject that is close to my heart. Bear with me now, as I attempt to clarify what has happened.

Yes, modesty is indeed a cornerstone of Jewish life. Women of the past scrupulously kept both *Dat Moshe* (the laws of modesty declared in the Torah) and *Dat Yehudit* (the traditional standards of modesty accepted by women through the ages).

The *Mishnah* states, for example, that Jewish women, through the years, avoided weaving in the marketplace. The *Gemara* explains why: The motions of weaving would cause them to expose their upper arms in public. This would be immodest.

Yes, our tradition of modesty is of the highest standard. How, then, can we explain its decline?

Well, dear Sarah, we can draw a parallel with one of the world's more interesting creatures, the chameleon. What does this creature look like? Well, it depends. You see, the chameleon possesses a unique ability. It can change its colors to match its surroundings. If it is perched upon a leaf, the chameleon can turn itself green. If it sits upon a twig, it can turn brown. On a rose, it can be red.

Many a human being, my dear granddaughter, is much the same. Not physically, of course, but in deeds.

People find it difficult to be different. Why, they feel, must *I* be the exception? Why should I not let my "colors" – my deeds, my outlook – conform to the environment which surrounds me?

Sarah, do you recall when, years ago, you and I read *Pirkei Avot* (*Ethics of Our Fathers*, an ethical tractate of the *Mishnah*) together? One of its directives, stated by the Sage

Nitai Ha'arbeli, is, *"Harchek mishachen ra* – Distance yourself from an evil neighbor" *(Avot* 1:7).

Today, Sarah, our neighbors are not limited to the people who physically live nearby. In the "global village" in which we live, our "neighbors" are everywhere, even great distances away. They include the people about whom we read in the newspapers. They include characters, even fictional ones, we "meet" through the media.

These neighbors may never bring us a cup of sugar, but they do bring us their thoughts, ideas, and values. And what values they have! The family, in their world, is an endangered species. Depraved lifestyles of entertainment people are matter-of-factly accepted. And fashion trends get progressively worse, with reckless disregard for decency.

Sarah, it hurts me to write this, but our girls, our women, have too readily accepted the influences of their global neighbors. Our strong tradition of modesty and the pristine simplicity of Jewish womanhood have been battered and bruised by the strong temptation to conform.

Is there any other way to understand the decline of modesty? Is there any other rationale for women — who have observed every *Shabbat* of their adult lives, who proudly send their children to *yeshivah* every morning, who would not even *consider* placing dairy food on a meat plate – wearing the clothing that they wear today?

Is there any other way to understand how Jewish wives and

mothers, fiercely independent in everything else they do, allow themselves to be sheepishly manipulated by designers of fashion, who decide for them what they should and should not wear?

And all this to what benefit?

Does a happily married young mother expect to enhance – or weaken? – her marriage by dressing immodestly before other men?

Does a young girl, seeking a level-headed, committed husband, who will build, with her, a model Jewish home, expect to attract him with indecent clothing? Will she not send better signals, and attract a better quality person, by maintaining her modesty and Jewish mode of dress?

Modesty, *tzniut*, offers us so much, and we must do our utmost to bring it back.

Sarah, there is much that you can do. First, maintain – even intensify – the commitment to modesty that you have now. Second, never, never let down your guard, never alter your "colors," chameleonlike, to match the colors of the world outside, to match the values of your global neighbors. And finally, take pride in what you have. Radiate commitment, *kedushah,* and tradition in every move you make, every word you speak, and, G-d willing, *be'ezrat Hashem,* we will return to our traditions of the past, and reverse the decline of modesty.

With love,
Your grandmother

Cliff Notes Generation

SHORTCUTS DO NOT WORK

Admit it. *You* did it, too.

You were assigned a book to read. It might have been *David Copperfield*. Or it could have been *Arrowsmith*. (I had a high-school teacher who said something like the following: "*Arrowsmith* is an excellent book. The only slow part of it is the first five hundred pages.") Or maybe *War and Peace* was your assigned book.

Your teacher had promised that you would learn a great deal from the book. Well, after a few tedious pages, there is one lesson that you *did* learn: *There was no way you were going to finish the book.*

So you went to the store and purchased *Cliff's Notes* (everybody called them *"Cliff" Notes*, without the apostrophe "s"). These brief pamphlets could summarize a 1,000-page book in only a few pages.

In any case, you ignored the original piece of literature which was assigned to you, even though it had been revered and acclaimed by literary scholars for generations – and shamelessly used the *Cliff's Notes* to complete your report.

Very often, you got away with it. The grade you received was acceptable or better. The shortcut, you felt, paid off.

You therefore became a member in good standing of the "*Cliff Notes* Generation." Your motto became: *Everything has a shortcut.*

∞∞

There is an interesting anecdote in the *Talmud* (*Eruvin* 53b), which sheds light on this matter.

> *Rabbi Yehoshua ben Chananyah said: "Once, I was walking along the road, and I saw a child who was sitting at a fork in the road. I asked him, 'Which is the road to the city?' He said, 'One road is short but long. One road is long but short.' I took the road that was short but long. Once I reached the [outskirts of the] city, I saw that there were gardens and groves surrounding the city [and I did not know how to get through them into the city]. I therefore went back. I said to the child, 'Did you not tell me that the road was short?' He said, 'Did I not tell you that it was actually long?' I kissed him upon his head and I said, 'Fortunate are you, Israel, that you are all wise, from your elders to your young.'"*

In life, we take shortcuts. We believe that they will get us to the "city" – help us to achieve our goals – through the shortest possible route. We have a subconscious belief – or maybe even a conscious one – that such shortcuts work. As members of the "*Cliff Notes* Generation," we feel that we can give less time to an important activity or project – and lose nothing by doing so.

However, just as a short pamphlet which summarizes a work of literature cannot bring you close to deriving the true flavor of that literary work, by the same token, many of the shortcuts we take fall far short of the desired result.

Take, as an example, time spent with children. There is a concept today called "quality time," as in, "you should spend *quality time* with your children." If this means that the time spent with children should be used as effectively as possible, then it is something good. If, however, it is understood to mean that you could spend less time with your children as long as you make that time "quality time," then you are taking a short road that is actually long.

Take, as another example, something from a totally different realm: prayer. What was prayer intended to be? The *Mishnah* tells us (*Berachot* 30b):

> *The early pious ones would tarry one hour and then pray, so they could properly direct their thoughts to their Father in Heaven.*

Before praying, one must do away with whatever thoughts are on his or her mind, and focus on the prayer to be said. Granted, due to the constraints of time, we may not be able to devote one hour to this purpose. We could, however, devote a few seconds in preparation before standing in front of our Creator.

Moreover, what about the prayers themselves? How many of us routinely rush through them? Is not a prayer uttered with sincerity and concentration far better than one rattled off in a way that leaves us no time to even think about what we are saying?

After all, at the end of our silent prayer, the *Shemoneh Esrei,* we recite this line:

> *May the utterings of my mouth find favor, as well as the stirrings of my heart, before You.*

"Stirrings of my heart?" This implies some feelings, some emotion, *some life!* When you rush through a prayer, barely getting the sounds out of your mouth, there is none of this. How effective could the prayer possibly be?

The shortcut you took did not get you into the city.

We take, as a final example, the study of Torah. When a man will stand in judgment (after his life is over), the question will be asked (*Shabbat* 31a):

> *Did you establish fixed times (kavata ittim) for the study of Torah?*

From the choice of words in the above question, our Sages

learn something important: The study of Torah must be the cornerstone of a man's schedule. Regardless of how little time a person spends in Torah study, he (we will discuss the woman's obligation afterwards) must make it the primary part of his day or week.

When a person does not take Torah study seriously – when he simply catches the tail end of a class as he is walking into synagogue, or comes to a class once then skips it three times – he is missing a great deal. He is, first, not giving Torah study the respect it deserves, and, second, is not fulfilling the obligation to make such study the cornerstone of his schedule. If he thinks this is an effective shortcut, he is seriously mistaken.

Although a woman's obligation to study is not the same as a man's, she does nevertheless have an obligation to study and must also give it the real commitment it deserves.

In view of what we have written, we must be aware of the following: We live in a generation in which shortcuts are commonplace. Mistakenly, many of us believe that we lose nothing by taking such shortcuts. We consequently devote little time to deeds, activities, and projects which actually require a great deal of time. Unfortunately, our lack of commitment is usually reflected in the results.

In whatever area of life it applies, be careful of the road you choose. It may look as if it is short – but it may actually be long. That shortcuts do not usually work is a lesson often lost on the *"Cliff Notes* Generation.*"

Kilroy Was Here

THE PERSON AND THE PRAYER ARE ONE

James J. Kilroy was a shipyard inspector. His job was to inspect barrels, bundles, and packages to be shipped to other ports. Upon the items he inspected, he would scrawl three trademark words to confirm that the product had been checked. As these items reached other ports, the three trademark words became famous:

Kilroy was here.

∽ ∾

When a person prays, he or she places a *personal trademark* on that prayer. The individual's attitude, sincerity, warmth, enthusiasm, and depth of feeling blend together with the prayer itself to produce something unique. *The magic of prayer comes as much from the person as from the prayer.*

This leads us to the following: A complex prayer that is uttered in careful detail, but is not backed by sincerity, carries little impact. On the other hand, a simple prayer, uttered by the right person at the right time, may indeed pierce the heavens.

The person and the prayer are one.

∽❧

The first recorded religious rituals in the Torah are the sacrifices of *Kayin* (Cain) and *Hevel* (Abel). Regarding this event, the Torah states (*Bereishit* 4:3-5):

> *And Cain brought an offering to G-d from the fruits of the land. And Abel, too, brought an offering from the first born of his sheep ... And G-d turned to [accepted] Abel and his offering. And to Cain and his offering He did not turn.*

A careful reading of this text uncovers an interesting choice of words. This text does not say: "And G-d turned to Abel's offering." Rather, it says, "And G-d turned to Abel *and his offering*." And the text does not say, "and to Cain's offering G-d did not turn." Rather, it says, "and to Cain *and his offering* G-d did not turn."

As Rav Ovadia Sforno notes in his commentary:

> *Abel was pleasing, as was his offering.*

And the reverse would hold true for Cain: Both he and his offering were unacceptable.

As we noted above regarding prayer: The person and the offering are one. The person who is insincere cannot separate himself, herself, from the prayer. One cannot, for example, flagrantly violate the moral and ethical codes of the Torah, yet expect some magical prayer to make everything good. On the other hand, the prayer of the sincere person, unsophisticated and simple as it may be, could have great impact.

The following incident, one of the many treasured tales of the Baal Shem Tov, illustrates the point:

A simple man found himself away from the city on Yom Kippur, and without a book from which he could read the prayer of this holy day. He said the following: *"Master of the Universe. You know the thoughts of man. You know that my desire is to thank You and praise You. However, I have no prayer book. I will, therefore, recite before You the letters of the Aleph Bet ... and I am certain that You will be able to organize them into the proper prayers and thoughts ..."*

Of this prayer, the Baal Shem Tov said, "Not in many years has a prayer of such purity ascended to the heavens."

Let us, then, remember the following: There is magic in prayer. But that magic comes from the person as well as from the words. You and your prayer are one. Your own trademark, your personal *"Kilroy was here"* is in every prayer you recite.

Eureka!

LEARNING FROM THE DEDICATION OF OTHERS

I would like to announce a discovery.

In any arena of life, role models play prominent parts in the lives of people. They set positive examples. They inspire. They make us strive to do more.

Spiritually, this is very much the case. When we see, hear, or read about extraordinary acts of righteousness, we often seek, in some small way, to emulate those acts. We become better people.

Where can you find these role models? How many individuals have you come across who exhibit a dedication to Torah that is so passionate and deeply felt that it ignites a fire inside you?

This is where our discovery comes in. As follows:

When Jacob, our forefather, returned from the house of Lavan, he sent word to Esau (*Bereishit* 32:5):

> *"I have lived [Hebrew: 'garti'] with Lavan."*

The word *garti* has a numerical value of 613. Based on this, *Rashi* elaborates on Jacob's words:

> *"Though I lived with Lavan, I did not learn from his evil deeds. I followed the 613 mitzvot."*

The message, based upon *Rashi*, appears to be: Though Jacob was in a hostile environment, he did not compromise. He kept the *mitzvot*. He did not learn from the evil deeds of Lavan.

The Maharam of Lublin, *zt"l,* however, understands *Rashi* differently. In his view, Jacob has regrets:

> *"Yes, I followed the mitzvot. But I did not fulfill my mitzvot with the same enthusiasm that Lavan had in performing his evil deeds."*

What a thought! Even individuals whose actions are unlike ours can teach us important lessons. Even if we have no interest in doing *what* they do, we would do well to learn *how they do it*.

Now, we can say the magic word: *Eureka!* What a discovery! We now have "role models" all around us!

Of course, we may not choose to do what they do. But you can't beat their enthusiasm.

❧❧

A case in point:

You awake early one morning. You are not certain about attending *minyan*. After all, it's early; it's still dark – who would go out at such an hour? You look out the window. There he is. A jogger! Then you see another one — and another one. *They* did not think twice about the time. *They* did not believe that 6 a.m. was too early to be out there.

I heard a similar story from an acquaintance:

He woke up one winter morning to find the city blanketed in snow. A fierce blizzard was raging outside. He decided to brave the elements and try to get to *shul* for his *daf yomi shiur*. He realized he would have to walk, as cars were buried in the white stuff, and besides, the roads were impassable. As he plodded through the knee-deep snow, shielding his face from the howling wind, he noticed someone else walking through the quiet, deserted streets. *Who else could be out in this weather?* he wondered. It was a man – walking his dog.

The joggers and the dog-walker felt strongly about what they were doing. They would not be deterred.

We can learn from them.

∽◦◦∽

Another case in point:

You happen to be in the office of a business associate, a product manufacturer. While you are there, this associate receives a call. As he speaks on the phone, you notice his excitement. His eyes open wide. His words are spoken with enthusiasm. His conversation is quite animated.

From the context of the conversation, you realize that the caller is a buyer for a large chain of stores. Your associate has never spoken to this person. The call is an opportunity.

Of course he's excited.

That night, your own telephone rings. It's a friend. He/she wants you to volunteer some time for an important project. This project will help your community. Your reaction when you discover the reason for the call? Lukewarm, at best. After all, you say, you are being asked for something. Should you be happy?

Yes! Learn from your business associate. Like the call which he received, the call to you is an opportunity. This is what we are here for! Your reaction should be: I live for this! There should be excitement in your voice. Your eyes should open wide. Your words should be spoken with enthusiasm. Your conversation should be highly animated.

Your business associate is a "role model." You should learn from him.

One more case in point:

Embarrassment: You are embarrassed to practice some *mitzvot* in front of other people.

There is no shortage of examples. You are embarrassed to wear a *kippah* (man); cover your hair (woman); eat kosher; dress properly; pray – or to do any one particular *mitzvah* in the presence of others who do not do them.

This, despite the words of King David (*Tehillim* 119:46):

> *"I will speak of your testimonies [the Torah] in front of kings and I will not be ashamed."*

Nevertheless, you are embarrassed.

Then you take a walk in the city: You see people from other countries, whose garb is quite conspicuous, freely walking about without hesitation or embarrassment. You see other people who have no qualms about following the latest trend: an earring in a man's ear; a woman with a nose ring or perhaps one on the tongue; maybe a middle-aged gentleman with a ponytail.

And you're worried about a *kippah!*

We do not, of course, desire to wear what those others wear. But there is something we can learn from them: the absence of fear and embarrassment.

Let each of us, therefore, examine his or her own dedication to Torah and *mitzvot*. If we find it to be lacking, we need only to look around. *Eureka!* You will discover many "role models" from whom you can learn.

Of course, we may not want to do what they do. But we sure can learn from *the way* they do it.

Spin

AVOIDING SELF-DECEPTION

Spin. At one time, this was its primary definition: *to rotate or cause to rotate.* Example: *I will spin the top.* Today, however, this word has taken on an additional definition: *to provide a positive meaning to an action or event*, as in the sentence: *Our public-relations people will put a positive spin on it.*

Spinning – as in the second definition – occurs all around us:

- An individual in government does something that is blatantly political. He gives it a positive spin, claiming he is doing it for the public good.

- A person in the public eye commits an indiscretion, or perhaps a crime. His spokesmen spin it in his favor.

- A professional athlete leaves his team to sign a lucrative contract with another club. His spinners insist that money is not a factor.

Of course, we have become accustomed to this. It is not convincing. We usually are not deceived.

There is *one* type of spin, however, which each of us finds to be quite convincing and which does indeed deceive us: *our own.*

⤶⤷

Each of us has a conscience. We believe that there is a Creator and that He has given us *mitzvot* to follow. We, of course, accept these *mitzvot* without reservation. We would never consider questioning the validity of even a single one of them. Our *thoughts* are good.

In practice, however, many of us are lacking in our observance. Some of the *mitzvot* are ignored. Some prohibitions are transgressed. Our *deeds* are lacking.

Question: How do we explain the contrast between thoughts and deeds? Should not our unease over failing to fulfill our responsibilities motivate us to change?

Answer: Ideally, it should – if it were not for *spin.*

With *spin,* we feel better. We can justify practically anything: *I did not know. I never learned. I am under financial pressure. Everybody does it. My husband or my wife would not understand. Some hold it's allowed. I am not capable of being better. It's a dog-eat-dog world.*

This spin is not for public consumption. There is nobody out there whom we must convince. There is nobody out there who has to be sold. *We spin our deeds to convince ourselves.*

What can we do to avoid this?

∞∞

We are all familiar with the story of Joseph and his brothers (*Bereishit*, Chs. 37-45): In Joseph's dreams, he saw his brothers bowing to him. He told his brothers of the dreams. Of course, they did not expect the dreams to come true. They were incensed at (what they viewed as) his arrogance. They sold Joseph into slavery. He was taken to Egypt where, eventually, he was elevated to a position of prominence.

Decades after they sold Joseph into slavery, his brothers came to Egypt, seeking respite from a famine. They indeed bowed to him, unaware of his identity. He finally revealed himself to them, saying, *"I am Joseph."*

The Torah then states:

> *His brothers could not answer him.*

Commenting on this dramatic confrontation, the Talmud states (*Chagigah* 4b):

> *When Rabbi Elazar reached this sentence, he cried, "'His brothers could not answer him!' If this is the reproach of a man of flesh and blood, how much*

more so the reproach of our Holy One, Blessed Is He
[on our day of judgment]!"

How do we explain the statement of Rabbi Elazar? What "reproach" is he speaking of? We do not see any words of reproach from Joseph to his brothers. "I am Joseph" is not a reproach.

This is correct. There were no words of actual reproach. Joseph did not say to them, "How could you?" or "You should have known better!" No matter. He did not *have* to say such words.

People who think, people of conscience, find their own reproach in what they see and hear. After all, until then the brothers had felt that the dreams had no substance. Now, " I am Joseph" proved that they were mistaken. Their thoughts, lasting many years, had clearly been proven wrong.

We turn back to the statement of Rabbi Elazar. He compared the reproach of Joseph to the reproach which *we* will confront on the day of judgment (after the life of each one of us is over).

How are they similar?

Well, as we noted earlier, many of us are less than perfect in our observance of Torah and *mitzvot*. By providing a positive spin to our actions, however, we justify our lack of observance.

On the day of judgment, the truth will be revealed. The equivalent of "I am Joseph" can, in an instant, obliterate our rationale for failure and bring the truth to light. It will cause even the *spinner* – the person being judged – to cease being deceived by his or her own words.

The Talmud tells us (*Shabbat* 31a):

> *Rabba says: "When a person is judged, they ask him, 'Did you deal honestly in business? Did you have a fixed time to study Torah?'"*

Though the person may have had a lifetime of experience in spinning, it will not help after 120.

Let us, therefore, not allow the *"I am Joseph"* scenario to take place. Let us now, and let us often, look closely at our lifestyle and at each of our actions. Let us re-examine our reasons for doing them. If we feel that we are being dishonest with ourselves – if we feel that we have put a positive spin on a negative action – let us change our ways and do better.

Spin may help politicians and athletes. It will not, however, help us.

In The Merit of ...

LEST OUR OWN MERIT NOT BE SUFFICIENT

*A*nswer us, our Father, answer us. Forgive our transgressions. Answer our prayers. And, lest our own merit not be sufficient, answer us in the merit of:

- those who came before us – our saintly ancestors, whose
  - piety had no bounds:
  - Abraham, Isaac, and Jacob;
  - Moses, the humble one;
  - Aaron, the peacemaker;
  - our holy Prophets;
  - the pious Sages;
  - righteous women, who formed the foundation of our people;
  - and all good people who came before us.

Answer us in the merit of:

- those who never lost faith;
- those who never swayed;
- those who gave their lives for Torah.

Answer us in the merit of:

- our parents – those who are here, and those who are not –
  - who put us at the center of their lives;
  - who lived with less so we could have more;
  - who taught us tradition;
  - whose words of wisdom ring ever so true.

In the merit of:

- the children:
  - who proudly recite the *aleph bet;*
  - who struggle with books that seem bigger than they are;
  - who keep little fingers firmly on the place;
  - whose innocence melts our hearts;
- the boy at *Bar Mitzvah. Today I am a man;*
- the bride, wide eyed, with hopes for the future. (Is that a tear in her eye?)

Answer us in the merit of:

- those who are immersed in Torah:
  - the teachers who instruct our children;
  - the rabbis who anchor our synagogues;
  - the *kollel* husband, the *kollel* wife, who teach us the meaning of sacrifice

Answer us in the merit of:

- the invalid, whose faith does not waver;
- the orphan, who has learned to be brave;

- the widow, who finds the strength;
- parents who have lost a child.

Answer us in the merit of:

- unsung heroes;
  - struggling wage earners who resist the temptation to work on *Shabbat*;
  - the peacemakers;
  - the matchmakers;
  - those who run from trouble.

In the merit of:

- people who give advice;
- people who take it;
- people who could flaunt, but don't;
- people who have conquered envy.

And answer us in the merit of:

- those who refine their character;
- those who control their tongues;
- those who hold no grudges;
- those who visit the sick;
- those who help the needy;
- those who conceal their good deeds.

Answer us, our Father, answer us!

- If not for our merit – for theirs.

Minding Your Own Business

GETTING INVOLVED

"He minds his own business."
Of the varied comments available to portray an individual, this one is considered to be among the more positive. Let's discuss it.

The following is a paraphrased excerpt from *Pirkei Avot* 5:13:

There are four types of people:

(1) One who says: *What is mine is mine. What is yours is yours*. This person is average, according to one opinion. According to another opinion, this person has the character trait of the *evil city of Sodom*.

(2) One who says: *What is mine is yours. What is yours is mine*. This person is an *am ha'aretz*. He is unlearned.

(3) One who says: *What is mine is yours. What is yours is yours*. This person is pious.

(4) One who says: *What is mine is mine. What is yours is mine.* This is an evil person.

Nearly all the comments of the Sages are readily understood, with the exception of: *"What is mine is mine. What is yours is yours ... This person has the character trait of the evil city of Sodom."*

The evil city of Sodom? Why? Understood, this person may not be the most *giving* individual in the world. But neither does he take anything that does not belong to him.

He simply minds his own business.

Why is this not acceptable?

Because it's not Jewish. In the city of Sodom, it was forbidden to help the poor. *We* cannot live that way. If a Jew simply does not hurt anyone – but does not help anyone either – he or she falls far short of the level that is expected of a good Jew. People need people. Those who are *able* to help must do so. *Minding your own business* is not good enough.

A while ago, two articles appeared in a daily newspaper.

One was in the business section. It was distressing. The subject: business failures. They were increasing. More and more firms were unable to stay afloat. The economy had taken its toll.

The other article appeared in the paper's main section. Its topic: a new sports car. The price tag: *over $60,000.* Yet the car was in huge demand! Dealers had waiting lists. They could easily sell the vehicle for more than its already hefty list price. Supply could not keep pace with demand.

Could this be? Some people frantically wait in line to part with thousands of their dollars — while others confront the unsettling prospect of living without an income?

At the same time? In the same place?

Yes, it could be. It always is. Some have more success than they ever dreamed of. And others struggle. *At the same time, in the same place.*

In microcosm, our own communities are much the same. Some people have enormous success. Others struggle. Often, the struggling is not anybody's fault. Some people may have had successful businesses, only to see them sink under the weight of a depressed economy. Others may have not yet found their niche, and are struggling to make ends meet. The effort is there. But the results have not come through.

Those who have succeeded are obligated to help those who have not. Those who can come to the help of others are not permitted to "mind their own business." They must become involved.

Now we may ask: Is there one particular character trait which moves an individual to become involved? Yes, there is. It's called *caring*.

The Torah states, regarding Aaron, the first *Kohen Gadol* (*Shemot* 28:30):

And Aaron will carry the judgment of the Children of Israel upon his heart.

Literally, "judgment" and "upon his heart" refer to the breastplate which Aaron wore. Figuratively, the commentary *Be'er Yaakov* (paraphrased) explains it this way:

> *Aaron would carry the judgment – in other words, the pain – of the Children of Israel upon his heart. If anybody was in pain, Aaron felt it. He would carry it upon his heart … and pray for that person.*

He cared.

We, too, are obligated to feel the pain of others. And we, too, are obligated to do what we can to alleviate that pain.

We can learn from this fable:

One day, in times of old, an eagle flew above the village. Suddenly, the eagle swooped down, lifted a young child from the ground, and flew off.

The horrified villagers watched as the eagle flew toward the mountains. Then it landed atop one of the peaks, loosened its grip on the child, and deposited it on the mountaintop.

Immediately, the villagers formed a search party. They headed toward the mountain, and began to climb. But the mountain was too steep. They were forced to turn back.

A while later, the villagers saw a sight which they could not believe. The mother of the child was descending the mountain – with the baby in her arms.

"You climbed the mountain?" they asked.

"Yes, I did," she replied.

"How could you climb the mountain, while we, stronger and more experienced than you are, could not?"

She answered, simply, "It's not your child."

When those who need help are close to us, we naturally make much effort to help them. It is as if it's "our child." When, however, it is somebody not so close, how much of an effort do we make on their behalf? After all, it's not "our child." How much do we care?

We must learn to care and we must learn to become involved. If we renounce this obligation, we have renounced a good portion of our Torah. Once we ignore our responsibility to those who have less than we do, we have retreated from the active role that Judaism challenges us to play. Once we've said, *"What's mine is mine; what's yours is yours,"* we've drained life of its excitement, its pulse, and its sense of worth.

Judaism challenges you to live your life by this principle. You must care for and about others. You must become involved. It's exciting, it's rewarding, and it's far more fulfilling than *minding your own business.*

Ushpizin

LESSONS FROM OUR ANCESTORS

According to the mystical teachings of the *Zohar*, every *succah* is visited by seven special guests (known as "*Ushpizin*"). These distinguished visitors – Abraham, Isaac, Jacob, Joseph, Moses, Aaron, and King David – grace the *succah* with their presence throughout the holiday. Each day, one of the seven leads the others.

I anxiously await the arrival of the *Ushpizin* – for their holiness, and for the lessons they can teach us. I have prepared welcoming words for each of them.

Welcome, Abraham. You are our first guest, as you were the first Jew. The idols you destroyed were not just those which were made of stone. You replaced cruel, pagan ideas with the holiness and morality of Judaism.

Teach us to be proud that we are Jews

- as you *called out in the Name of G-d* in your travels;

- as you proudly declared your Jewishness;
- as you firmly made known your beliefs, despite an environment which was alien to them.

Teach us, please, to do the same. Teach us to be proud. Teach us to withstand the intimidation of those who have alien ideals. Teach us to stand tall, and to proudly *call out in the Name of G-d* by observing our cherished *mitzvot* — no matter *how* they may seem to the world outside.

Abraham, our father, please teach us.

Welcome, Isaac. You are the second of our three forefathers. You are the son of Abraham. You are the father of Jacob.

> *Teach us to pass on our traditions to the next generation.*

Regarding the wells you dug in the land of *Pelishtim*, the Torah says (*Bereishit* 26:18):

> *and he called them by the same names that his father did.*

Is this not a lesson for us? Much of what we must accomplish has actually already been done. If we can simply *rediscover* the heritage of our fathers, if we can *reaffirm* our traditions – we will have achieved a great deal.

Teach us, then, to be a link between the past and the future, as *you* were.

Welcome, Jacob. You are *Israel*. Every Jew bears your name. *Teach us to acknowledge what G-d has given us.* You said (*Bereishit* 32:11):

> *"I am made small [humbled] by all the acts of kindness ... which You have done ... for with [only] my rod I crossed this Jordan [River], and now I have become two camps."*

You recognized that you had prospered.

Teach us, please, to do the same. Teach us to compare what we *were* to what we *are* — what we had before to what we have today.

Teach us to acknowledge how much we have. Teach us to say, "*I have been made small.*"

Welcome, Joseph. You were sold into slavery as a teenager. Your brothers turned against you.

Teach us how to forgive — as you forgave. Your words to your brothers, putting them at ease, were (*Bereishit* 45:8):

> *"You did not send me here [to Egypt]. G-d did."*

Could we learn to be as forgiving? Could we learn to overlook the wrongs that are done to us by others? Must we hold our grudges until the end of time?

Teach us, Joseph, to forgive.

∞∞

Welcome, Moses. You are *Rabbeinu*, our teacher, the Lawgiver.

Teach us to be humble.

Regarding you the Torah states (*Devarim* 34:10):

> *And there has not risen in Israel a prophet again like Moses.*

And (*Bamidbar* 12:3): *And the man Moses was more humble than any man upon the face of the earth.*

Though you reached the pinnacle of greatness, your humility remained. Cannot we, then, far from perfection as we are, find it within us to come down from our pedestals? Can we not cease looking condescendingly at those around us? Can't we infuse some humility into our lives?

Teach us, Moses our Rabbi, our teacher.

∞∞

Welcome, Aaron. You are our first *Kohen Gadol.*

Oh, Aaron, your visit is quite timely. What *you* have, *we* need – desperately.

Teach us to love peace.

Our Sages said of you, *"Oheiv shalom, verodeph shalom."* You loved peace, and worked diligently to achieve it. You brought people together. You turned enemies into friends. You made peace between people who were in conflict.

Aaron, we know a few people in conflict with others. Aaron, we know *many* people who are in conflict with others.

Teach us, please, to bring peace between them.

And finally: *Welcome, David, our king.*

Teach us, please, what it means to be a friend.

Your relationship with your friend, Jonathan, is acclaimed by our Sages (*Avot* 5:16):

> *Love that has no ulterior motive: That is the love of David and Jonathan.*

Can this be taught? Is it possible that *we* can be sincerely devoted to *our* friends? Can we learn to be sincerely happy when they do well, and to be genuinely in pain when they suffer?

Please, our king, teach us to be so.

Yes, I anxiously await the arrival of the *Ushpizin*. I have much to say to them. And there is so much that they can teach us.

Rooms

THE IMPACT OF "SMALL" DEEDS

He was given two keys.

One was the key to a *huge* room. He opened the door and entered the huge room. Then he walked through the room and opened another door, which took him into a smaller room. He walked through this second room and opened another door. *This took him into a room that was smaller still.*

Then there was the other key. It was a key to a *small* room. He opened the door and entered the small room. He walked through the small room and opened another door, which took him into a larger room. He walked through this second room and opened another door. *This took him into a room that was huge.*

In effect, the first key, which was a key to a *huge* room, led him eventually to a room that was actually small. And the second key, which was a key to a *small* room, led him eventually to a room that was actually huge.

∞∞

The first key, which opens the door to the huge room, represents much of the allure of this world. Very often, as we pursue the mundane attractions of this world, we believe them to be of great consequence. If, however, we follow these attractions to where they lead us, we are disappointed. *The key to the huge room leads us to a room that is quite small.*

The second key, which opens the door to the small room, represents spiritual activity. It represents our *mitzvot,* the beloved commandments which we follow. Often, in carrying out a *mitzvah*, we believe that we are doing something of little significance. If we follow this *mitzvah* to where it leads us, however, we discover that it is quite more far reaching than we ever imagined. *The key to the small room leads us to a room that is quite large.*

In *Pirkei Avot* 2:1, it is stated:

> *Rebbi said, "Be as careful with a 'light' mitzvah as with a 'heavy' one – because you do not know the relative rewards of the mitzvot."*

A *mitzvah* may seem to us to be "light" – only to lead us to something that is much greater. Its "reward" may be nothing less than a major breakthrough in a person's life.

A student misbehaved in yeshivah,* and the principal was

* *The story of the boy in yeshivah was told by Rabbi Paysach Krohn in a speech.*

about to expel him. The young man cautioned the principal, "You can expel me if you like. Realize, however, that in doing so you are not only expelling *me* – you are expelling my children and my children's children as well." The principal relented and allowed the student to remain in the school.

The young man made a valid point. To deprive him of a Torah education is to deprive future generations as well. To *provide* him with a Torah education, on the other hand, is to provide it as well to the generations which follow.

One action would have enormous effect.

We are reminded of a *Midrash* (*Shemot Rabbah* 1:33) about Moses:

When the Jewish People were enslaved in Egypt, the Torah relates (*Shemot* 2:11-12):

> *[Moses] saw an Egyptian man beating a Hebrew man ... And he looked here and there and saw that no man was present – and he slew the Egyptian and buried him in the sand.*

The *Midrash* tells us: He looked "here and there" – he looked (with prophecy) *into the future*. He looked to see if, in future generations, any "man" was present – if any offspring of merit would be born from that Egyptian. Only after he was certain that no good people would be among the descendants, did he go ahead and slay the aggressor.

An action could be much more negative than we think it

is – as Moses feared his action might be. On the other hand, an action could be much more positive than we imagine it to be.

We must, in effect, *look into the future* before acting, and consider the far-reaching effects of our deeds. The impact of what appears to be a minor *mitzvah* may be far greater than we imagine.

Many people are under a mistaken impression. They feel that people's lives are most affected by dramatic turning points – by big, bold events that change the course of people's lives. For the most part, this is false. Many of the milestones of life are small, seemingly insignificant events that lead to other events that finally make their mark.

In *Imrei Shefer,* by Rabbi Shmuel Pinchasi, it is noted (we paraphrase): *Physically*, the human body is composed of myriad tiny cells. By the same token, *spiritually*, we are what we are because of myriad tiny milestones, which together make us the people we are.

A life scenario:

- A man begins attending morning prayers in synagogue. He has no dramatic plan to overhaul his life; he simply makes a decision to attend daily prayers. One morning, an evening class is announced. It is "worth a try," so he attends. He enjoys the class, and continues to attend. Through the class, he becomes much more committed to Judaism – and his life is transformed.

Did this person, originally, make a conscious decision to turn his life around? Absolutely not. However, one step led to another, and the result was one of major significance.

The small "room" led into something quite large.

Another life scenario:

- A young man's parents accede to their son's request. He would like to continue his Jewish studies. As a result, not only does the young man grow in Torah knowledge and in commitment – he also becomes a stabilizing force in his family and an inspiration to his brothers and sisters.

A third life scenario:

- A woman decides to become more involved in helping others. She begins working with a young mother in crisis. Gradually, the young mother comes out of her difficulty. She becomes a better mother and a better wife. Her children grow up well, marry good people, and raise good families of their own.

Helping one person, in effect, helped many.

We therefore cannot take any *mitzvah* for granted. We must be as careful with a "light" mitzvah as with a "heavy" one. We do not know to what glorious destination the *mitzvah* will take us.

That key may lead you to a room that is not small at all.

"Quack, Quack," Said the Eagle

RAISING OUR SIGHTS

In a towering tree above the forest, there was an eagle's nest. One day, while the mother eagle was away, a fierce wind pounded the forest. It shook the tree and its branches. An egg fell from the nest and landed, incredibly, in another nest, down below. This nest, however, was not a nest of eagles. It was a duck's nest.

The mother duck did not notice the new arrival. Unknowingly, she sat upon the eagle egg, together with her ducks-to-be.

Soon the eggs hatched. Out came a number of newborn ducks — and one newborn eagle.

The newborn eagle did not know what he was. He looked at his "siblings" and thought that he was one of them. Like the little ducks, he would fly only a few feet above the ground. He became one of the group.

"Quack, quack," said the ducks.

"Quack, quack," replied the eagle.

One day, a flock of eagles flew overhead. They spotted the young eagle, and asked, "What are you doing down there? You should be up here, soaring above the trees with us."

The young eagle replied, "I belong here. I'm not an eagle – I'm a duck."

With coaxing, the eagles were able to convince the young eagle to attempt to fly, as an eagle should. Slowly but surely, he flew higher and higher, eventually soaring through the skies at great heights. He was, indeed, an eagle.

⟐

We are "eagles." We are people of the spirit, people of *kedushah*, holiness, people with higher goals. The Torah elevates our lives. It makes us soar. It states (*Shemot* 19:5):

> *And you will be unto Me a treasure among the nations.*

However, we look at the world around us – and we see "ducks." Pick up any newspaper, any day, and read all about it: corruption, deceit, dishonesty, marital infidelity, greed, selfishness, and lack of principle. These traits are displayed, not only by criminals and social misfits, but also by individuals who are very much in the public eye.

Consequently, people lower their sights. They are content to be like the other people in the world around them – or perhaps a bit better than they are. They tend to think that they are ducks.

"Quack, quack," said the ducks. "Quack, quack," replied the eagle.

We must understand what we are. We must realize that other people are not a frame of reference for us. Being *like* them, or even a bit better than them, is far from enough.

Stand apart. Put *kedushah* into your life. Don't stay down with the ducks. Soar the heights with the eagles.

Imagine

ASPIRATIONS

*I*magine ...

- if we could, just for a few moments, stand again at Mount Sinai;
- if we could catch just a glimpse of the Splitting of the Sea, or the manna falling in the desert;
- if we could capture the inspiration and store it, drawing upon it always, to keep us strong;

Imagine ...

- if we could have one more chance with the *Bet HaMikdash*, our Holy Temple, to see if we can keep it standing, and not destroy it with petty hatred, as we destroyed it last time.

Imagine ...

- if we could put our ears to the door of an ancient House of Learning, where the Sages of the Talmud were engrossed in study, where the animated give-and-take shook the walls to their foundations;

- if we could have a fraction of their knowledge;
- if we could have a taste of their dedication.

Imagine ...

- if we could return to simpler days:
  - if "the Joneses" drove only a Chevrolet, and lived in a three-bedroom apartment;
  - if the next *brit milah* we attend is not as elaborate as a *bar mitzvah*;
  - if the next *bar mitzvah* we attend is not as elaborate as a wedding;
  - if the next wedding we attend is not as elaborate as a coronation.

Imagine ...

- if the legendary community leaders of yesteryear had the affluence of today to work with.

Imagine ...

- if we could follow every dollar of charity to its ultimate destination:
  - if we could see the poor child eating the food; the needy immigrant wearing the clothes; or the bricks being laid upon the wall of a building which our funds helped to purchase.

Imagine ...

- if we could speak – please, just for a minute – with parents and grandparents who have left us — to tell them that we love them — to ask for their counsel — and to tell them that time has proven them right.

Imagine ...

■ if we could take back all the time we wasted. We know now how to use it;

■ if we could return to the yeshivah or *ktab* of our childhood — to study Torah with the clear mind of a child, knowing what we know now about its importance.

Imagine ...

■ if we could take back all the words we uttered in anger. We didn't mean them;

■ if we could strike from the record our insensitive remarks – to our parents, to our spouse, to our children, to friends. They deserve much better.

Imagine ...

■ if we could take back:
  • the prayers we recited without concentration;
  • the *Shabbatot* we spent without holiness;
  • the holidays we spent without enough joy.

Imagine ...

■ if we can draw upon the mistakes of the past — to rise to new heights in the future.

Just imagine ...